X-PLANES 15

COLD WAR DELTA PROTOTYPES

The Fairey Deltas, Convair Century-series, and Avro 707

Tony Buttler

SERIES EDITOR TONY HOLMES

OSPREY
PUBLISHING

OSPREY PUBLISHING
Bloomsbury Publishing Plc
PO Box 883, Oxford, OX1 9PL, UK
1385 Broadway, 5th Floor, New York, NY 10018, USA
E-mail: info@ospreypublishing.com
www.ospreypublishing.com

OSPREY is a trademark of Osprey Publishing Ltd

First published in Great Britain in 2020

A catalogue record for this book is available from the British Library.

ISBN: PB: 9781472843333; eBook 9781472843326;
ePDF 9781472843340; XML 9781472843357

20 21 22 23 24 10 9 8 7 6 5 4 3 2 1

Edited by Tony Holmes
Artwork by Adam Tooby
Index by Alison Worthington
Originated by PDQ Digital Media Solutions, UK
Printed and bound in India by Replika Press Private Ltd

Osprey Publishing supports the Woodland Trust, the UK's leading woodland
conservation charity.

To find out more about our authors and books visit www.ospreypublishing.com.
Here you will find extracts, author interviews, details of forthcoming events and
the option to sign up for our newsletter.

Acknowledgements

I would like to thank the following for
their vital contributions to this work,
both with reference materials and
illustrations – Gerry Balzer, Bob Bradley
(San Diego Air & Space Museum), Bill
Harrison, Phil Butler, Henry Matthews,
RAF Museum, Mark Nankivil (Greater
Saint Louis Air & Space Museum), Brian
Riddle (National Aerospace Library),
Tommy Thomason, the staff of the
British National Archives at Kew.

Front Cover

For the September 1956 SBAC
Farnborough Airshow it was intended
to display the Fairey Delta 2's speed
capability to the public. WG774 and
WG777, flown by Fairey chief test pilot
Gp Capt Gordon Slade and his deputy
Lt Cdr Peter Twiss, respectively, would
essay a supersonic cross-over directly
above Farnborough at 38,000ft (visible
to the public by their contrails), and in
doing so produce level-flight sonic
bangs which at this time had not
previously been publicly demonstrated
in Britain – these would be audible on
the ground some 25 seconds later.
During practice their routine went
smoothly, but unfortunately it never
happened during the airshow itself
because of inclement weather.
(Artwork by Adam Tooby)

Previous Page

Delta 2 WG774 banks away from the
camera to reveal its famous delta
planform during a pre-SBAC
Farnborough Airshow air-to-air
photography flight in September 1957.
So many of Britain's research and
experimental aircraft were only ever
seen in public at Farnborough, which
explains why most of them were
photographed just before, or during,
these hugely popular – and important –
airshows. (Author's Collection)

X PLANES

CONTENTS

CHAPTER ONE

FAIREY DELTA 1

The arrival of the jet engine towards the end of World War II as a new power source for fighter-type aeroplanes offered designers previously unheard-of possibilities in terms of speed and performance. Once the new technology had matured, the power produced by the jet would see fighters (and later bombers and airliners) exceed not just the speed of sound but more than twice that figure. Such speeds had been simply impossible with piston power, but a further element was needed to get full value from the jet – advanced aerodynamics. Fortunately, this too was on hand, in particular in the form of the swept and delta wings.

The aircraft industry worldwide took on both configurations, but in the 15 years immediately after World War II some manufacturers put their faith in the swept wing, while others selected and stayed with the delta. During the 1950s the primary fighter design bureaus in the Soviet Union, Mikoyan and Sukhoi, both produced leading supersonic designs with delta wings, while in France, Dassault created a string of highly successful delta-wing fighters and bombers with its Mirage series.

In Britain, Gloster Aircraft fitted its Javelin nightfighters, and Boulton Paul its P.111 and P.120 research aircraft, with deltas. However, the British company to put the most investment into this platform in terms of high performance aircraft was Fairey Aviation. In America, the lead exponent of the delta was to be Convair, and this book looks primarily at the programmes of these two manufacturers, which in many respects followed quite similar paths but resulted in entirely different outcomes.

Both companies began with subsonic designs, both at some stage produced a rocket fighter, and the main objective of both was to create

Delta 1 VX350 in flight on 14 September 1953. The short, stocky, appearance of the aeroplane is most pronounced when viewed from this angle, and at one stage *Flight* magazine described the aircraft as 'projectile-like'. The horizontal 'torpedo' fairings of the original swivelling pipe arrangement aft of the wing had been replaced by smaller and neater trailing edge fillets by the time this photograph was taken. (Author's Collection)

a top-class interceptor. In the end Fairey broke the world air speed record with its Delta 2, but politics then blocked the path and the firm never fulfilled its desire to build a production jet fighter. Convair experienced huge aerodynamic problems with its early F-102 Delta Dagger airframes, but eventually large numbers were built and the type was succeeded by the far more capable F-106 Delta Dart. Convair also produced a flying boat jet fighter.

One further manufacturer to take the delta on board 'in full' was the British Avro company, but here it was chosen as the platform for a bomber, what became the Vulcan. Avro decided that the delta would be ideal for providing a strong and solid wing to carry a large nuclear store to a height of some 50,000ft whilst cruising at a high subsonic Mach number. Here, supersonic speed was not a factor but rather the delta's ability to provide lift. However, in the late 1940s, the unknowns of this planform still needed to be assessed, particularly its low-speed characteristics. Avro duly built a series of 707 aircraft specifically with this research in mind. The Avro 707s are covered in the final chapter, and make an interesting comparison to the high-speed research undertaken by Fairey and Convair.

THE DELTA WING

A pure delta wing is essentially a triangle and gets its name from the Greek alphabet's uppercase letter delta, which has the shape of an equilateral triangle ('delta' designs would also encompass layouts with clipped wingtips and slightly swept trailing edges). As a planform, the delta provided an ideal combination with the jet since it offered good flight characteristics for high subsonic, transonic and supersonic flight. Its structure was also relatively easy to build and was in general stronger, stiffer and lighter than a swept wing offering a similar amount of lift. And since it inherently had more internal volume than a swept wing, the delta also provided more space for fuel and equipment without incurring a penalty in drag.

A further advantage was that the relatively low thickness also reduced wave drag (a component existing only when supersonic airflow was present), giving the delta particular appeal for supersonic flight. It was also naturally stable in pitch and so did not require a separate tailplane. Finally, as the delta's angle-of-attack (AoA) was increased, its leading edge would generate a vortex that helped to energise the uppersurface flow, thereby making possible a very high flight angle at the stall. In these early days of jet aircraft research, a swept wing designed for high speed could be dangerous at low speeds, but the delta at these low speeds was helped by the additional lift that came from this vortex.

However, swept wings possessed a better lift-to-drag ratio than the delta wing, and high-lift devices such as Fowler flaps proved difficult to integrate into the delta planform. Also, fighter-type delta wing aeroplanes would lose energy very rapidly in turns, which put them at a disadvantage in air combat when high manoeuvrability was required. Thus, the delta wing was more suited to interceptors designed to attack bombers, rather than for pure dogfighting aeroplanes.

The true pioneer of the delta as a practical wing for aeroplanes was German designer Alexander Lippisch, who began evaluating this wing shape after World War I. He flew his first research aircraft (the Delta I) in 1931, and by the start of World War II was working with Messerschmitt, where he contributed much to the design of the Me 163 Komet rocket-powered interceptor. In 1943, Lippisch moved to the Aeronautical Research Institute in Vienna to concentrate on the problems associated with high-speed flight, and here he produced a design for the delta-winged Lippisch P.13a supersonic fighter, which was to be powered by a ramjet – the aircraft never flew. After the war Lippisch went to America to continue his research, and one company to benefit from this would be Convair.

Separately, in America, Robert T. Jones of the *National Advisory Committee for Aeronautics (NACA)* Langley Research Center had been working on a theory that thin-aerofoil delta wings would prove superior for supersonic flight (to date Lippisch had concentrated on much thicker delta wings). Jones's work was eventually published in January 1945, and it paved the way for practical delta wings for supersonic flight. His theory was accepted in the summer of 1945 after Robert Gilruth and Theodore von Kármán had conducted tests with models in a supersonic wind tunnel, and after the discovery of wartime German research.

EARLY BRITISH EXPERIMENTS

In December 1946, Fairey's Stockport facility in Greater Manchester designed a pilotless delta wing rocket-powered model called the HALA. A full-size research aircraft project called the Type R soon followed, and this was proposed to the Ministry of Supply in February 1947, with the model programme to provide back-up data. In September, Specification E.10/47 was issued to cover the Type R project, and on 19 April 1948 a contract was awarded for three aeroplanes carrying serials VX350, VX357 and VX364. Eventually, the new type was named 'Fairey Delta' (and subsequently Delta 1 with the arrival of the aircraft in the next chapter).

The Delta 1 was an exceptionally small single-seat aircraft, and it was intended to perform research at high subsonic speeds and with high-angle ramp launching. A tailless aeroplane, it would assess the control and stability problems produced by the delta wing. For ramp launching it was intended to have an engine jet pipe split into four exit branches, with each branch terminating in a swivelling end, universally mounted and connected to the pilot's controls. This arrangement would allow the jet efflux to be deflected, thereby providing control about all axes during the initial stages of a ramp launch (when the normal aerodynamic controls would be ineffective because of the aircraft's very low speed).

The ramp launch idea was soon dropped and the Delta 1 would operate with a conventional undercarriage and a simple single jet pipe. The lobes that had been built into the rear fuselage to

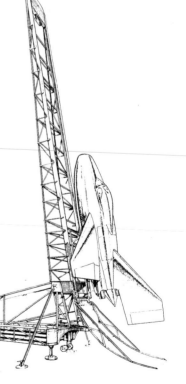

The Delta 1 was originally intended to take-off using a launch ramp, as per this sketch from the original Fairey brochure. This rather uncomfortable-looking approach was soon abandoned. (Author's Collection)

The Delta 1 was taken off the Secret List by the Air Ministry on 14 March 1951, just two days after the aircraft had made its maiden flight. This angle shows the faired-over horizontal lobes that were to have formed part of the split jet pipe for ramp take-offs. Throughout its career VX350 sported a highly polished metal finish.
(Author's Collection)

house the split jet pipe were thus faired over and, prior to first flight, a brake parachute was installed in the lower jet pipe lobe.

Built in conventional light alloy with frames and stringers, the Delta 1's wing was clipped at the tips to permit streamlined fairings to be fitted. The aircraft's controls were fully power-operated using Fairey-type control jacks, and there was provision for manual reversion and artificial feel was provided. The rudder was of a conventional type, but the wing controls were elevons (combined ailerons and elevators) and fitted with trim tabs. The airbrakes were located at the wing trailing edges between the fuselage sides and the inboard ends of the elevons. These were of the counter split type, and could be opened progressively up to the aeroplane's maximum design speed of 650mph Equivalent Air Speed (EAS) – the basic aircraft was designed for a dive speed of 650mph or Mach 0.95, whichever was the lower.

For early flights only it was decided to fit a small fixed tailplane on top of the fin and also fixed wingtip slats, the former to increase the damping in pitch and the latter to reduce any wing-dropping tendency near the stall. The slats were subsequently removed, but the tailplane remained throughout VX350's career.

The Delta 1 was 26ft 3in. long, its wingspan was 19ft 6.5in., the wing was swept 40 degrees at quarter chord, it had a relatively high thickness/chord ratio of ten per cent and the gross wing area was 155.7sq ft. Maximum take-off weight was 6,769lb, which included 130 gallons of internal fuel, and the powerplant was a single 3,500lb thrust Rolls-Royce Derwent 5 engine.

In 1951 Fairey told the aeronautical press that the Delta 1 had been designed for 'important research work with revolutionary possibilities in the design and operation of fighter aircraft'. However, by late 1950, work on the second aircraft, VX357, was virtually at a standstill –

FAIREY DELTA FD 1

This three-view depicts the Delta FD 1 VX350 as it was
displayed at the SBAC Farnborough Airshow in September 1954.

the fuselage was structurally complete but its wings were still in their
jigs. VX357 finally received its Derwent engine in January 1951, but
it would never fly. The part-complete third Delta 1, VX364, was
cancelled on 11 January 1950.

FLIGHT TESTING

Delta 1 trials flying was the responsibility of Fairey chief test pilot
Gp Capt Gordon Slade and his deputy Lt Cdr Peter Twiss. VX350
was assembled at Fairey's Heaton Chapel, Stockport, facility and taxi
trials began, well behind schedule, on 12 May 1950 at Manchester
Ringway Airport. After being moved to the Aeroplane and Armament
Experimental Establishment (A&AEE) at Boscombe Down, Wiltshire,
taxiing resumed on 1 September, but this was stopped again by
hydraulic problems. It was January 1951 before the trials restarted.

In a short hop made on 21 February Slade achieved unstick at
155mph, and then on 12 March 1951 he took VX350 on a 17-minute
maiden flight from Boscombe Down. By 20 September only 3.5 hours
had been accumulated in ten flights, and then the aircraft suffered a
landing accident and flying ceased for some time. VX350 was, however,
statically displayed at the September 1951 Society of British Aerospace
Companies (SBAC) Farnborough Airshow.

In April 1953 Fairey summarised the flying completed so far, even
though VX350 had not flown for some 19 months. Problems during
flight testing and then the accident meant that the Delta 1 had flown
far less than planned. In addition, the longest flight had lasted just
25 minutes, and on one occasion only four gallons of fuel remained
in the tank on landing. However, this limited endurance was in part
due to the fact that all flying so far had been undertaken at heights
below 10,000ft. The present limiting speed of 345mph EAS had been
achieved on just one occasion.

X PLANES
FAIREY DELTA FD 1

After the first flight Slade reported a powerful low-speed lateral oscillation. He stated that 'within a second of unstick and without conscious movement of the control column, one wing moved sharply down 15 to 20 degrees [and] instinctive correction toppled the aircraft the other way equally sharply. These lateral oscillations continued irregularly to a greater or lesser degree, but always jerkily at the rate of rather more than one a second'. In fact, the oscillation continued with varying severity right through the flight, but was less marked on the approach after the airbrakes had been extended. During the second flight the lateral oscillation was still present, but was less severe, and Slade reported that he felt it was initiated by bumps. He also confirmed that extending the airbrakes increased the damping of the oscillation.

Modifications made to the aileron control reduced the initially severe lateral oscillation. The aircraft remained in this condition for the rest of its flight testing, and eventually the oscillation came to be regarded as a nuisance rather than a severe handling difficulty. Sometimes VX350 would fly perfectly steadily, then suddenly the oscillation would commence without any warning. Cessation of the motion occurred with equal suddenness, sometimes with the control column free and sometimes when the ailerons were being used in an attempt to damp the motion. Generally, the oscillation occurred more frequently in rough air conditions and appeared to get worse as VX350's speed was increased. Extending the airbrakes appeared to have a beneficial effect, and fortunately the oscillation never occurred during the approach – at a time when, of course, the airbrakes were generally extended. On one occasion the approach was made with the airbrakes closed, and again the aircraft was quite steady, but in this particular case the air conditions were also calm.

Despite the aircraft having the wingtip slots and tailplane fitted, up to the maximum 345mph limit, the longitudinal stability had been satisfactory and very stable in all flight conditions. The lateral handling characteristics, however, were described as like being balanced on a knife edge – indeed the aircraft was very sensitive in the roll, and with the engine throttled back the rate of sink became very high. This was caused by the aircraft's high density and possibly also by the large size of the fuselage relative to its wing. The knife-edge stability and high sink rate therefore made the approach on landing a tricky, if not dangerous, business.

Generally, with the control column free, the nose wheel would lift off at

This air-to-air view shows the aircraft's large air intake and substantial cockpit canopy in relation to the rest of the airframe. The pilot, however, still had pretty cramped accommodation. Seen here in late August 1954, the Delta 1 was almost certainly undertaking a photographic sortie so that the press could see it in the air during preparations for the SBAC Farnborough Airshow, held in early September. The latter event provided the aircraft with its only opportunity to fly in front of the public. (Author's Collection)

In this view of Delta 1 VX350 (taken while on static display at the 1954 SBAC Farnborough Airshow), the modified rear fuselage, jet pipe and parachute fairing are well shown. In the early 1950s, this was the smallest jet-powered aircraft in Britain. Note the leading-edge slats and the wingtip excrescences, the latter housing anti-spin parachutes – these were later replaced by a housing positioned underneath the jet pipe. The aeroplane carried no weaponry. (Author's Collection)

around 103mph. As the incidence was increased slightly at 161 mph, the aircraft would unstick cleanly and smoothly and without any longitudinal pitching. The tailplane undoubtedly contributed much to these satisfactory characteristics, in that when it was set at a negative angle of 5.5 degrees it caused the nose to rise gradually at small elevator angles. This avoided a necessity common on other tailless aircraft types of needing a large elevator application to lift the nose followed by a rapid control column reversal to check the pitching motion.

In the absence of a crosswind, VX350's take-off characteristics were satisfactory, the aircraft almost flying itself with only light control inputs. However, in crosswinds of even moderate strength, the take-off was not so straightforward. Side forces on the aircraft, combined with its narrow-track undercarriage, caused a list to develop on the runway. If the ailerons were used to correct this, a sharp and disturbing wing drop would occur as the main wheels left the ground. In these circumstances Slade found it advisable to leave this list uncorrected and then unstick with the control column free in the aileron sense. The climb away proved satisfactory, and the acceleration and the climbing angle could be controlled by the throttle with ease. An extension of the airbrakes to moderate and maximum angles produced a nose-down change of trim, but the required corrective movement of the elevators was small.

Including some circuits and bumps, 14 landings were made. Slade had established that the best technique was to start the approach at a speed of 184mph with the airbrakes extended, slow down to 172mph on nearing the end of the runway and then hold off at 161mph. The touch down, with the tail skeg just clear of the ground, would take place at 155mph, with little weight on the main wheels over about the first 250 yards. The brake chute had usually been streamed immediately after each touch down, and Slade commented that the resulting deceleration had been 'very reassuring'.

FURTHER ASSESSMENT

On 23 November 1951 Air Ministry officials and Fairey's new Technical Director and Chief Engineer, Robert Lickley, discussed the Delta 1's unpleasant handling characteristics. In addition to the comments previously outlined in this chapter, Lickley added that VX350's rate-of-climb had proven to be less than the original estimate because of the aircraft's excessive weight (the Delta 1 was 2,600lb heavier than the original estimate). Sink-rate, high wing loadings

and low endurance were all
features of new jet aircraft
designs, but on the Delta 1
they were compromised by
its poor handling. In fact, by
the time Lickley met with the
Air Ministry, VX350 had been
deemed 'a dangerous aircraft'
and grounded.

Company Chairman Sir
Richard Fairey had also become
very concerned about the
Delta 1's flight characteristics
and had ruled that Fairey would no longer work on the aeroplane.
His attention was now firmly on the supersonic Delta 2, although
both technical issues and cost had influenced his decision to end the
Delta 1's development.

The Delta 1 touches down at the
SBAC Farnborough Airshow in
September 1954. All of VX350's test
flying was conducted from either
Boscombe Down or Farnborough. After
the airshow, *Flight* magazine
commented that 'while a high rate of
roll is somehow expected of such a
machine, the example given during
Tuesday's flying display proved almost
unbelievable – even to those who saw
it.' Note here how close the rear
fuselage is to the ground.
(Author's Collection)

During the period when VX350 was grounded, Royal Aircraft
Establishment (RAE) Farnborough, in Hampshire, analysed the
airframe very closely. As a result, action was taken to clean up the
airflow over the rear fuselage, and the two horizontal lobes from
the original 'swivelling' jet pipe were renewed and faired off. When
flight testing recommenced, it was hoped that the various modifications
would improve the handling characteristics.

VX350's flight trials finally resumed on 5 June 1953, and by
12 August a total of ten hours of flying time had been accumulated.
The Delta 1 was now accepted off contract from Fairey to the Air
Ministry and returned to the A&AEE at Boscombe Down for its
official trials. Here, the fixed leading-edge slats were removed, after
which VX350 at last became a useful research tool for examining the
behaviour of delta-winged aircraft in general. Pilots still preferred to
fly this particular aeroplane in good weather conditions, however. An
increasing understanding of low-speed handling permitted the type's
rolling characteristics and its lateral and longitudinal stability to be
examined with confidence.

The sole Delta 1 performed its first public flying display at the 1954
SBAC Farnborough Airshow, where its phenomenal rate of roll and high
landing speed left a big impression. Then, on 6 February 1956, VX350
suffered an accident at Boscombe Down that brought an end to its
flying career. Sqn Ldr Dennis Tayler, a test pilot making a familiarisation
sortie in readiness to fly the Delta 2, found the undercarriage would
not lower properly as he made his landing approach. The nose leg came
down, one main leg dropped partially and the other did not drop at
all. On landing, Tayler veered off the runway onto the grass, badly
damaging VX350. It was duly deemed not worthy of repairing. On
9 October 1956 the Delta 1 was taken away for use as a weapons
target at Shoeburyness, in Essex. This odd little aeroplane had not
proved very successful, and in its career had accumulated only a modest
number of flying hours over a long period of time. The maximum
speed it achieved in flight was 397mph.

CHAPTER TWO

FAIREY DELTA 2

WG774 and WG777, flown by Fairey chief test pilot Gp Capt Gordon Slade and his deputy Lt Cdr Peter Twiss, respectively, line up on the famous Farnborough runway threshold 'piano keys' in September 1956. Once aloft, they would essay a supersonic crossover directly above the airfield at 38,000ft, producing level-flight sonic bangs in the process. This photograph was taken prior to Slade and Twiss undertaking a practice flight of the routine, which would have been a highlight of the airshow that year had the display not fallen victim to the inclement weather.
(The Aviation Historian)

The Fairey Delta 2 was a supersonic research aircraft designed to investigate the flight characteristics of a delta planform with 60 degrees of sweep on the wing leading edges when flying at speeds well above Mach 1. The two examples built and flown proved to be invaluable research tools over a long period of time and, in addition, in March 1956 the first Delta 2 broke the world air speed record in one of the finest achievements in British aviation history.

In mid-1948 the Air Ministry raised an unofficial requirement for a single-seat supersonic research aircraft. Seven manufacturers submitted designs, and those subsequently turned into hardware were the English Electric P.1 (flown in 1954 and later developed into the Lightning Mach 2 fighter) and the Fairey Delta 2. Fairey's initial proposals were ready in September, and they showed an aircraft quite like the P.1 with extreme sweepback on its wing and tail. However, in 1949, the firm began to investigate low aspect ratio delta wings, and, in due course, a 60-degree swept delta wing layout was produced which the firm labelled Type V.

A proposal for an all-moving T-tail for the Type V was made in July 1950. By early January 1951 the project was close to what was eventually built, except for the T-tail, which added 200lb to the structure weight and increased the all-up-weight from 12,535lb to 12,650lb. However, on 8 May 1951, Fairey reported that incorporating the tail incurred a major stiffness problem on the fin structure and gave a large amount of drag. The centre of gravity had moved aft by six inches and, although the weight penalty was not prohibitive, it was vital to save weight on this aircraft. The tailplane was thus deleted on 18 May.

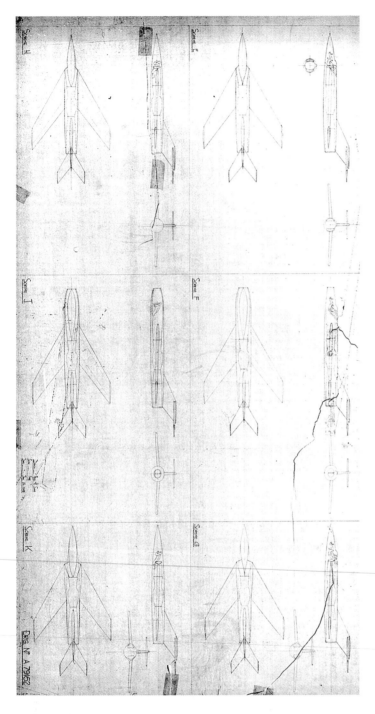

This original Fairey drawing shows six different concepts for a supersonic aircraft, all of which were eventually discarded in favour of the delta wing. The document illustrates how the company began with layouts based on lines proposed by RAE Farnborough, before moving on to its own ideas. As such, it reveals the design processes that can occur with a new aircraft type. The drawing is dated 26 January 1949. (Author's Collection)

RIGHT
The first Delta 2, WG774, displays its sleek airframe during the early part of its flying career, and while still in bright natural metal finish. The aircraft had yet to break the world air speed record when this photograph was taken. Its wing was of true delta form, wind tunnel testing having exceeded 1,000 hours before the final shape was confirmed. There was no tailplane. (Author's Collection)

Two aircraft (serials WG774 and WG777) and a static test specimen had been ordered in 1950, and specification ER.103D was raised around the new type (numerous published sources state ER.103D also covered the P.1, but its specification was F.23/49 that included armament). Fairey's aircraft was apparently officially designated FD.2, but to the manufacturer it was known as the Delta 2.

In June 1957 Fairey proposed an ER.103D variant with an extended fuselage and 70-degree delta wing. Span would be 25ft 5in. and length 52ft 7in. For performance purposes, an aerodynamic ejector convergent-divergent nozzle was assumed, which gave the basic 70-degree delta conversion a reheat-unlit top speed of about Mach 1.7 in clean condition. At 36,000ft the level acceleration from cruise at Mach 0.93 up to Mach 1.8 would take just 1.35 minutes, while at 45,000ft the estimated time was 2.65 minutes. The available research time at supersonic speed when flying in the 40,000 to 55,000ft region was predicted to be 17+ minutes at Mach 1.5 and more than 11 minutes at Mach 1.8. (Author's Collection)

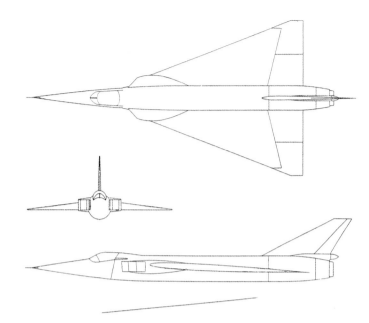

STRUCTURE

Fairey's design team was led by chief engineer R. L. Lickley, while the chief designer was H. E. Chaplin. Dr H. F. Winny looked after aspects such as flutter and the aircraft's airworthiness, which involved calculations in realms never previously explored. Chaplin was

This extremely unusual view of WG774 was taken during the aircraft's approach to land following a flying display at the September 1955 SBAC Farnborough Airshow. Note how slim the tyres are on the main undercarriage wheels. (Author's Collection)

responsible for many of the Delta 2's best features, including the droop nose and the stowage of the main undercarriage within what was a very thin wing. When the latter was designed in 1949, its four per cent thickness/chord ratio was the lowest yet achieved in Britain and the lowest known anywhere.

In fact the Delta 2's design broke much new ground in fields for which there was very little experience and flight data available at the high Mach numbers expected (in the behaviour of the engine and air intake system, for example). In addition, the Delta 2 introduced duplicated fully powered controls with no means of manual reversion – in other words, the pilot's control column served purely as a selection lever to a system of valves. This was a novel feature in the early 1950s, but by 1957 had become standard for new aeroplanes.

The light alloy fuselage showed an almost constant section for some 30ft, the frontal area was kept as small as possible, and the finely tapered nose and long probe could tilt downwards hydraulically through ten degrees from a point to the rear of the cockpit. This gave the pilot a much better view during taxiing, take-off and landing. The centre fuselage consisted of heavy frames connected by longeron members, the frames absorbing the wing loads and supporting the Rolls-Royce Avon RA.14R of 9,500lb of thrust dry and 14,500lb with reheat. Structurally, the lateral air intakes were relatively simple (the saving in weight over a nose entry was proven to be worth more to the design than any aerodynamic problems they might create), although the engine bay had a number of auxiliary intakes. The rear fuselage was of monocoque construction and had petal airbrakes mounted at the end.

The wing was made of light alloy, with stressed skinning over three main and two supplementary spars. Perpendicular spars were

The Delta 2's lead test pilot for manufacturer's trials flying was Lt Cdr Peter Twiss, who also used the aircraft to break the world air speed record. He had been a successful fighter pilot in World War II, serving with the Fleet Air Arm. (Author's Collection)

employed, with the ribs or stringers running parallel to the fuselage centreline since this reduced the spar length and simplified the attachments to the fuselage frames. Horn-balanced ailerons were fitted and the powered flying surfaces stretched the full length of the trailing edge, with the inner surfaces serving as elevators. There was a single large fence positioned well inboard on each wing.

The twin-wheel nose leg folded rearwards into the fuselage and the main undercarriage (made in steel and fitted with very thin wheels and high-pressure tyres) was stored entirely inside the wing. Particularly heavy design-loads were imposed by this undercarriage which made necessary the employment of very thick wing skins and heavy forgings. The wing was also sealed to permit it to be used for integral fuel. The fin featured a three-spar structure and the rudder was also power-operated. Delta 2 had a span of 26ft 10in., its length was 51ft 7.5in. and gross wing area 360sq ft. Maximum weight was given as 14,531lb.

FLIGHT TESTING

Building the two airframes was delayed because Fairey's production capacity was fully taken up urgently constructing Gannet anti-submarine aircraft for the Royal Navy. Although a full size mock-up was examined officially on 27 June 1951, construction of the first airframe did not begin until late 1952. WG774 was finally completed in mid-1954 and was then taken by road from its Hayes, Middlesex, birthplace to A&AEE Boscombe Down. There, on 6 October 1954, Peter Twiss took it on a 25-minute maiden flight.

Twiss was pleased with the handling characteristics, and on succeeding flights the maximum speed was gradually increased until Mach 0.9 was recorded in November. However, on the 17th of that month, the Avon engine cut out at 30,000ft. Fortunately, Twiss was able to glide back and make a successful 'dead-stick' wheels-up landing at Boscombe Down – an achievement which brought him the Queen's Commendation for Valuable Service in the Air. WG774's damage was such that it had to be returned to Hayes and have the starboard wing replaced by the wing from the static-test specimen. Flying did not restart until 5 July 1955, with a sortie made from RAE Bedford, near Thurleigh in Bedfordshire.

When flying resumed the Mach number was increased, and the first transonic and supersonic runs were made on 28 October 1955 following a shallow dive starting at 35,000ft. Such was the smoothness of the transition that, after a mild nose-down trim change at about Mach 0.95, there was no indication that the Delta 2 had passed from high subsonic into supersonic flight except by referring to the instruments. This early supersonic flying was conducted entirely without using reheat, as dry thrust was sufficient to take WG774 up to Mach 1.1. Indeed, Twiss found that Mach 1.2 could be recorded in a slight dive without trouble – this figure was approaching the world air speed record, and yet reheat had still to be introduced.

When the Avon's reheat was lit, Twiss found that the acceleration it provided was 'an embarrassment to accurate flight test results, which gave the pilot a feeling of loss of control'. In fact, if reheat was lit in the climb, it proved difficult to avoid exceeding the air speed and Mach number at which flutter tests had so far been conducted, so the speed had to be held when the correct height was reached in readiness for the next set of tests. In truth, the pilot 'could not keep the Delta 2 slow enough even in the climb!' If reheat was used, sorties were usually limited to just 20 to 25 minutes of flight time. Nevertheless, much valuable data was being accumulated, no mechanical issues had been experienced with the power controls, and at times two, three and even four flights a day were being made.

SPEED RECORD

It was becoming clear that the Delta 2 could easily set a new world air speed record, beating the 823mph held by Col Horace Hanes in a North American F-100C Super Sabre. It was the ease with which the aeroplane passed into the supersonic regime, with none of the violent behaviour experienced by other types in the transonic region, that made this such an obvious step. Mach 1.56 was reached in November, and the flight team realised that the record could go beyond 1,000mph. Once the planning for the record attempt was under way, everything was kept as secret as possible to the point where the cover story proved so effective that many engineers were unaware of what was happening until shortly before the attempt began.

Since WG774 was again based at Boscombe Down, the decision was made to lay out a flight course across West Sussex between Chichester and the Royal Navy base at Ford – ground observation and recording sites were set up at both locations. The flying height was fixed at 38,000ft because this approximated to the level for optimum performance, and also ensured a good contrail (the latter was essential for ground tracking). For previous record attempts using subsonic (i.e. Mach-limited) aeroplanes, it had been necessary to fly in hot weather conditions to reduce the Mach number appropriate to a given airspeed. For the Delta 2, however, the coldest atmosphere was needed in order to increase the thrust of its engine.

Extensive telephone services were set up by the General Post Office and plugged straight into lines laid down for a now disused airfield. In addition, two complete installations of the most advanced British Army radar were made available. Gloster Meteor NF 11 nightfighters of No. 29 Sqn took off each day to assess the true contrail height, calibrate the radars and check the communication systems, and during the Delta 2's flights a specially calibrated de Havilland Venom measured the height as WG774 flashed by. The ground radar would vector the two aeroplanes into the best positions, but getting WG774 into the right place and height at the right moment called for meticulous timing and superb piloting skills. By 7 March everything was in place and ready for 'Exercise Metrical'.

Between 7 and 10 March, in superb weather for the time of year, Twiss made nine flights, but on each sortie either technical problems with the ground equipment or some other factor prevented a new record from being set. He always took off on a westerly course and followed a route designed to make the best use of the fuel load. A climb was made over the New Forest, and then reheat was lit and the aircraft's acceleration made continuous from here until the run ended. Reheat was cancelled after the eastward pass and a wide 180-degree turn made over the sea, before Twiss brought WG774 back in to repeat the whole procedure in a westerly direction. A minimum-power let-down ended in a landing at Boscombe Down after approximately 24 minutes flying time (following the record run Twiss landed without enough fuel to make an overshoot and another approach).

At last, a tenth flight, which started at 1121hrs on 10 March 1956, yielded the results that secured the record – speeds of 1,117.6mph and 1,146.9mph on the two runs gave a mean figure of 1,132.1mph. This equated to 983.7 knots Indicated Air Speed (IAS) and a mean Mach number of 1.731 (a maximum of Mach 1.8 was recorded during the flight). Peter Twiss had increased the world air speed record by no less than 37 per cent, WG774 having flown at a speed in excess of Mach 1.6 for 2.8 minutes. The aeroplane was still accelerating at the end of each run.

When the record was announced on 11 March the popular press went crazy. Worldwide, the record produced quite an effect, and in general it was received with great enthusiasm. The Air Ministry's Stuart Scott-Hall was in the USA when the record flight took place, and he found the Americans gave generous acclaim to the achievement. He thought it true to say, however, that 'they were quite astonished. For months they had been reading that the British aircraft industry had failed to produce the goods in this direction and in that. They would have had good excuse for thinking that the British were in a bad way. The capture of the record gave the British aircraft industry a tremendous uplift, while Americans concerned with high-speed aircraft development, no matter what type of wing they favoured, swept wing, straight wing, or delta, appeared to be equally surprised at the performance achieved.'

A few days later, when the press arrived at Boscombe Down, WG774 was being serviced and so the second Delta 2, WG777, had its fuselage serial number quickly changed to WG774 in readiness for the cameras. Fairey intended to display the aircraft's speed capability to the public at the September 1956 SBAC Farnborough Airshow. WG774 and WG777, flown by Slade and Twiss, would essay a supersonic cross-over directly above Farnborough at 38,000ft (visible to the public by their contrails), and in doing so produce level-flight sonic bangs, which at this time had not previously been publicly demonstrated in Britain (these would be audible on the ground some 25 seconds later). During practice for the display, their routine went smoothly, but persistent wet weather prevented the Delta 2s from performing this unique routine during the airshow itself.

On 12 December 1957 the USA reclaimed the record with a speed of 1,207.6mph set by a McDonnell F-101A Voodoo.

SONIC BOOM PROBLEM

Regular supersonic bangs produced over the speed record course during the attempt, and thus heard near the same places, brought numerous complaints. In fact, there was growing concern countrywide about the effects of supersonic bangs, and the Delta 2's flying programme was effected by widespread reports of this 'nuisance' and by the restrictions which were imposed on all supersonic flying over Britain (no supersonic flight was allowed below 30,000ft).

The whole time an aircraft flies at supersonic speed it produces an intense pressure wave that may result in a bang, or bangs, being heard on the ground. A Mach angle forms in the path of the aircraft, and this angle when the machine is travelling at Mach 1.0 is 90 degrees to the aircraft's direction. However, as the aircraft's speed increases so the angle is reduced and, three-dimensionally, the well-known supersonic cone appears which advances at the speed of the aircraft.

The intense pressure or shock waves that supply the bang to the human ear form at right angles to the Mach angle, so when the aircraft is at Mach 1.0 these travel in the same direction as the aircraft. But, as the speed approaches Mach 1.5 and beyond, and the Mach angle is reduced, the shock waves form in a direction that is heading towards the ground. Indeed, at this point, the path of the shock waves towards the ground from an aircraft in level flight is quite steep. At Mach 2.0, or if the aircraft goes into a dive, it gets even worse.

Wind, temperature, aircraft attitude and longitudinal accelerations affect the shock wave's path, but altitude has the greatest effect on the severity of the pressure change, or bang, and thus any damage it may cause. Considerable attenuation takes place at any distance from the aircraft, so the higher the aircraft is flying the less powerful the bang is at ground level, to the point where it becomes more of a rumble. Although it was difficult to predict the damage caused by supersonic bangs in 1956, during the speed record runs one Hampshire nurseryman reported more than 300 windows shattered in his greenhouses. The problem for Fairey was that the Delta 2's low-level

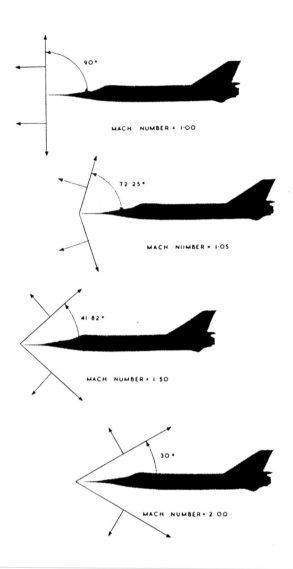

This illustration shows the development of shock waves with increasing Mach number. (Author's Collection)

supersonic performance had still to be investigated, but now there appeared to be nowhere suitable to do it!

In the meantime, WG777 had begun its flying career on 15 February 1956, again with Peter Twiss in the cockpit. The second machine showed slight differences in equipment and instrumentation, and the underwing flap system had been removed, but otherwise it was identical to WG774. Powered by an Avon RA.28 giving 9,300lb thrust dry and 13,100lb with reheat, WG777 joined RAE Bedford on 18 April. On 13 June 1956 WG774 flew three interceptor demonstration flights at the Fighter Convention held at the Central Fighter Establishment (CFE) at West Raynham, Norfolk – the first time such a type had been available to provide ground controllers with experience of handling supersonic aeroplanes.

Over the next few years the two aircraft were flown on research programmes both by the manufacturer and by the RAE's Aero Flight at Bedford. These programmes were complimentary, but with a little overlap, Fairey concentrating on clearing the aircraft through its flight envelope, the functionality of its fuel, hydraulic, electric and pneumatic systems and the pressure cabin, plus flutter systems and engine performance, plus some research. This also included the engine-intake combination, which, as noted, had been taken up to Mach 1.8. Aero Flight concentrated on the measurement of longitudinal and lateral derivatives, thrust and drag, and other associated aspects.

FRANCE

A venue for supersonic flight at lower altitudes was finally found when agreement was reached with the French authorities to fly from the *Armée de l'Air* air base at Cazaux, in southwest France. This area had a good weather record compared to a typical British autumn, and was reasonably sparsely populated. On 11 October 1956 WG774 flew from Bedford to Cazaux, and in four-and-a-half weeks completed 51 flights before returning home on 15 November. A considerable extension of the flight envelope was completed and valuable practical information on the intensity of sonic bangs on the ground was obtained. Both the engine and reheat system were worked hard and a very large number of selections made.

Supersonic runs were carried out at 5,000ft intervals from 30,000ft down to 15,000ft, and then at 2,500ft intervals from 15,000ft down to 3,500ft. The Mach number was increased in increments at each height, and at 25,000ft and Mach 1.5 the spread of the bang was considerable. As the height was reduced the spread became less until at 5,000ft and Mach 1.125 the tracking sites heard only a rumble. Twiss flew all but five sorties, the remainder being performed by Gordon Slade.

One discovery made in France were the handling difficulties experienced by the pilot when the Delta 2's transonic trim changed. Although this had previously been considered mild, Twiss noted that the change which occurred at Mach 0.95 became more marked as the IAS was increased. During a rapid acceleration with reheat, the nose-down pitch was uncomfortable and the resulting negative g sufficient to starve the reheat fuel supply, which resulted in an immediate

cancellation of reheat. Deceleration below Mach 0.97, if made without correction, could result in a nose-up trim change, giving +4g, which, if made rapidly, was most uncomfortable and often resulted in pilot-induced oscillation. This trim change had become a most unpleasant feature, and artificial 'feel' for the powered controls was now seen as an important additional item.

In the very smooth weather conditions over France, advantage was also taken to make some high-airspeed manoeuvres, which included turns of up to 4g at Mach 0.9 at 2,000 to 3,000ft. Supersonic manoeuvring was limited by elevator jack stalling, and the maximum g that could be applied dropped from approximately 3g at 20,000ft and Mach 1.3 to 0.75g at 3,500ft and Mach 1.05. There was never any buffeting or instability during these supersonic manoeuvres. The rolling performance remained good up to the highest speed/Mach number combination tried, and a few 360-degree rolls were made to obtain accurate rates of roll at both sub- and supersonic speeds. A rate of 250 degrees per second was attained on some high subsonic rolls.

After the French trials the aircraft received extensive modifications. Then, between 19 August 1957 and 4 March 1958, 59 flights were made in Britain which covered preliminary work on a convergent/divergent reheat nozzle, 'zoom climbs' to higher ceilings and a second set of CFE trials in December. A number of climbs beyond 50,000ft were made using a technique where the aircraft was accelerated up to the tropopause at a relatively high Mach number, pulled up 2–3g in a 20- to 30-degree climb and held at that angle until the desired altitude was reached; reheat was selected for as long as possible. A maximum 55,000ft at Mach 1.25 was achieved after reheat was cancelled at 52,000ft and the aircraft continued to zoom for several thousand feet. The CFE trials were conducted in collaboration with the Royal Radar Establishment to assess supersonic interceptions – a fighter aircraft capable of intercepts at speeds above Mach 1 was of course not yet available.

When WG774 was repainted for the 1957 SBAC Farnborough Airshow, it had the titling *HOLDER OF WORLD ABSOLUTE SPEED RECORD* applied along its forward fuselage. The mauve/pink scheme was, in the author's opinion, an awful choice of colour for this (or any other) aeroplane. From this angle, three of the six auxiliary intakes on the sides of the Delta 2's engine bay can be clearly seen. (Author's Collection)

In 1958, plans were made for an Avon engine development programme that required supersonic flights at a range of heights up to 40,000ft. The 30,000ft limit for British supersonic flight would prevent much of this work from being completed, and this time the French could not help. However, the Royal Norwegian Air Force (RNAF) offered airspace over Hardangervidda – a vast, wild and sparsely populated mountain plateau area northeast of Stavanger. This proved to be near ideal, and the facilities at the neighbouring RNAF base at Sola were good too. On 5 June 1958, WG774 flew to Sola, from where low-altitude supersonic trials took place between 5 June and 2 July. A total of 20 flights were made from Sola, covering the envelope between Mach 1.25 at 7,000ft to Mach 1.6 at 40,000ft. Three flights were also made above 40,000ft before WG774 returned to Bedford on 2 July.

PROPOSED DEVELOPMENTS

Fairey produced two different proposals to try and extend the aeroplane's research capabilities, neither of which was taken up. In July 1955 a brochure was prepared for the 'Type V' (Delta 2) fitted with two 16in.-diameter ramjets as supplementary power units to the Avon RA.14R, which would increase the aircraft's speed up to Mach 1.8 (this was before Fairey had discovered the full speed capability of its aeroplane). There was also a need for a suitable vehicle on which to test these ramjets, and the Delta 2 seemed attractive for the purpose. The best position for installing the two units was underneath each wing just outboard of the chassis, the ramjets raising the maximum level Mach number by 0.3 to 0.4, dependent on altitude, and the maximum supersonic ceiling by 6,000ft.

In June 1957 Fairey proposed a modified research aircraft which was a basic Delta 2 fitted with a more powerful engine and the facility to accommodate an extended wing with a 70-degree sweep leading edge. Fairey noted that the planned workload for both prototypes was so heavy that they were likely to be fully engaged for at least the next two years. There was thus little possibility of extending the development work to embrace an increase of either aircraft altitude or speed unless a third prototype was constructed.

By modifying the fuselage and fitting an Avon RB.133 (which had a greater mass flow than the current RA.14R), the operating speed could be raised to Mach 2.2 (the strength limit of the airframe) and the operating altitude to 60,000ft, with appreciably increased supersonic duration. The 70-degree wing would also allow the examination of the new problems expected with more highly swept deltas. Essentially a standard Delta 2 airframe would be built, but with its 60-degree wing interchangeable with the new 70-degree version. When fitting the latter, the common cockpit, centre and rear fuselages would be retained, but a new intermediate rear fuselage section would be inserted in the region of the 60-degree wing's trailing edge.

FAIREY DELTA FD 2

Delta FD 2 WG777 was painted in this overall dark blue scheme during its time with RAE Bedford's Aerodynamics Flight.

FINALE

Besides Norway, WG774's tasks during 1958 included measuring the control angles required in trimmed manoeuvring flight, position error at high altitude, measuring steady rates of roll, pressure measurements around the leading edge of the wing, measuring boundary layer thickness at the rear fuselage and flight clearance of a large ventral tank (of which photographs are very rare).

In 1959 WG774 performed a nozzle trials programme which involved fitting (in turn) a National Gas Turbine Establishment (NGTE) ventilated convergent-divergent nozzle, a Rolls-Royce ejector-type nozzle and a Rolls-Royce fixed convergent-divergent nozzle, the latter serving as a performance reference. WG774 joined RAE Bedford on 1 May 1959, it was loaned to NGTE on 7 May and began the programme on the 13th. This was concluded in December after 56 flights, which had included supersonic level runs at speeds up to Mach 1.78.

In September 1959 it was agreed that the Delta 2 could serve as an infra-red target for a de Havilland Comet operated by de Havilland Propellers, with the latter measuring the Delta's infra-red radiation when flying at height using supersonic shock-wave and infra-red measurement and detection equipment. These flights were part of the development programme for the new Red Top air-to-air missile, and through spring 1960 WG774, with the original eyelid exhaust nozzle back in place, conducted flypasts with the Comet, overtaking the larger aircraft at different speeds to enable variations in readings to be recorded.

WG774's Delta 2 career ended on 5 September 1960 with Flight 503 – a ferry trip to Filton in readiness for its conversion into the BAC 221 high-speed Ogee-wing trials aircraft for the Concorde development programme. As the 221, it first flew on 24 April 1964 and completed another 288 flights before the aircraft's final retirement on 4 June 1973. WG774 is preserved in the Fleet Air Arm Museum at Yeovilton, in Somerset.

X PLANES
FAIREY DELTA FD 2

In 1957, WG777 was used for aerodynamic tests at supersonic speeds, the work also embracing lateral stability, performance, pressure plotting and kinetic heat trials. WG777's 1958 programme included the measurement of thrust and drag throughout the aircraft's Mach range, wing pressure plotting, an examination of dynamic stability, the study of buffet at subsonic and transonic speeds, measurement of wing and fin loads with strain gauges, and kinetic heating on the wing. Pressures caused by supersonic bangs on the ground were also measured.

WG777 flew extensively during the second half of 1961 but did not fly from December of that year until November 1963. In 1964 it conducted assessments of vortex pressure fluctuations, Dutch roll trials were performed in 1965 at speeds up to Mach 1.8 and wingtip parachute trials were undertaken in spring 1966. WG777's 429th, and final, flight took place on 13 July 1966, and today it resides in the RAF Museum at Cosford, in Shropshire.

An unusual view of WG774 at RAE Bedford in May 1959 fitted with a NGTE ventilated convergent-divergent nozzle, ready for assessment trials against other nozzles designed by Rolls-Royce. (Author's Collection)

ASSESSMENT

In June 1956 WG774, with an RA.28 engine installed, was flown twice by veteran World War II fighter ace Wg Cdr Harold Bird-Wilson. He reported that the Delta 2 had extremely responsive and crisp controls, the best yet fitted to a British aircraft and the nearest to the ideal system that he had yet flown. Pilots liked the immediate response and smoothness of the controls in the American F-86, F-100 and F-102A, and Bird-Wilson noted that these were features 'badly lacking in types like the [Hawker] Hunter and [Supermarine] Swift'.

General handling was carried out at around 36,000ft, and during accelerated runs without reheat the Delta 2's transonic characteristics were described as most mild and superior to the USAF's F-86E, F, H and D, the F-84F, the F-100A and C, and the F-102A. While accelerating from Mach 0.9, no trim change was noticed until Mach 0.96

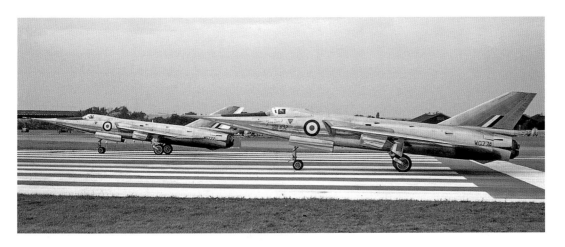

WG777, seen here in 1961 at Farnborough, was rarely photographed. This was probably because the aircraft spent most of its time in Air Ministry hands, preventing it from attending many airshows. Flight reported that at an open day at RAE Bedford in early July 1957, WG777 produced 'a goodly double sonic boom' and displayed a new dark blue high-speed paintwork experimentally applied to the fuselage aft of the hinging nose. By 1961, and by then the only surviving Delta 2 (WG774 having commenced its conversion into the BAC.221), the livery was dark blue all over. (Terry Panopalis Collection)

was reached, where a slight nose-down trim change occurred that could easily be held on the elevator and quickly trimmed out. As speed increased through Mach 1.0, the nose-down trim continued but, after the initial correction, level flight could be maintained without high stick forces.

The Delta 2 was the first aircraft Bird-Wilson had flown that could go supersonic without afterburning – the F-100 and F-102A were both subsonic until the afterburner cut in. Without reheat, WG774 was found to accelerate smoothly and quickly in level flight to approximately Mach 1.05. As the afterburner lit, the pilot felt 'a distinct thump and the acceleration is outstanding', and reaching Mach 1.25 was a 'most exhilarating feeling with no noticeable flight phenomena'.

On his second flight, Bird-Wilson lit reheat at Mach 0.88 and accelerated to Mach 1.57 in just 2.3 minutes. The acceleration was 'extremely smooth' and, once the transonic trim change had been trimmed out, he was impressed by the performance and, again, by the responsive controls throughout the speed range. While decelerating in manoeuvring flight from supersonic speed, a pitch-up occurred at around Mach 0.96, which, once the pilot was familiar with it, became unnoticeable from the tactical aspect. The petal-type airbrakes were extended only at Mach 1.0 at 30,000ft and at 345mph at 10,000ft, and they provided satisfactory deceleration without any apparent longitudinal trim change or adverse buffet.

Bird-Wilson concluded that in the Delta 2, Fairey had produced a very fine design and a wonderful piece of engineering. High Mach number speeds were reached without any of the adverse transonic or supersonic characteristics usually so pronounced in aircraft when approaching these speeds. The 'ingenious' method of drooping the nose was also a great help to the pilot's visibility during landing.

RAE pilots, however, have indicated that the Delta 2 was not so easy to fly, demanding constant attention at subsonic speeds and being even trickier in the transonic region, proving difficult to trim laterally and conveying an impression of continuous Dutch roll. Pilot John Humphreys observed that 'Peter Twiss did a wonderful

job of taking the absolute speed record the way he did because the aircraft was not easy to fly accurately, and to make two opposite direction runs and keep within the strict height allowance during the whole period was a brilliant achievement.' Fuel was also very limited (approximately 2,400lb), and 'if the wind at Bedford meant taking off from the far side of the field, we always got a tow to the take-off point and started up there. As a research aircraft for high Mach numbers the saving grace, quite apart from its performance, was its steadiness once supersonic.'

The highest speed recorded was Mach 1.82 (on 27 January 1959) at about 37,000ft. The author has been told that time-to-heights were not measured in detail, but 0 to 40,000ft in four minutes was possible with reheat.

Persistent high Mach numbers gave high skin temperatures and were also liable to soften the Perspex canopy panels.

The two Fairey Delta 2s proved to be extremely valuable research tools, experiencing long and immensely successful careers and gathering tremendous supersonic knowledge. Known to pilots as 'The Fred', the Delta 2 was a superb achievement. Once in the air, it needed little in the way of design changes – a remarkable fact when one considers the great advances required in technology and aerodynamics to facilitate production of the aircraft. The Delta 2 was not built to set records, and yet it will always be remembered for breaking the world air speed record in such a spectacular manner.

The droop nose, undercarriage doors and end fuselage petal airbrakes are all well shown in this shot of WG774 taken just after touch down at the September 1956 SBAC Farnborough Airshow (the nose undercarriage doors had to be opened to permit the nose to drop). The aircraft is still in natural metal, and carries *Fairey Delta 2 WORLD SPEED RECORD 1132 M.P.H.* titling on the droop nose immediately beneath the cockpit. (Author's Collection)

CHAPTER THREE

FAIREY ROCKET FIGHTER AND 'DELTA 3'

This manufacturer's artist's impression of the enormous Fairey 'Delta 3' long-range interceptor appeared in the design's project brochure, submitted in October 1955. The aircraft is shown carrying Red Hebe missiles (a development of the Vickers Red Dean) and wearing the false serial ZA538. (Author's Collection)

Fairey put a lot of effort into creating a production fighter or interceptor based on its Delta 2 for RAF service. These attempts are reviewed briefly here, and, although the final design for a long-range interceptor nearly got there, in the end the only 'fighter-type' jet aircraft built by the firm were the Delta 1 and two Delta 2s. Three aeroplanes seems a pretty poor return for the effort Fairey put into its high performance aircraft programmes.

ROCKET FIGHTER

In January 1952 the Air Staff of the RAF issued Specification F.124T, which requested a rocket-propelled interceptor to provide a last-ditch defence system against incoming enemy aircraft flying at height. Prime requirements were an outstanding rate of climb (sea level to 60,000ft in 2.5 minutes) and supersonic speeds at all heights above 30,000ft. The aircraft was to be armed with de Havilland Blue Jay (Firestreak) air-to-air missiles or 2in. air-to-air rockets. Six manufacturers submitted designs, with two coming from Fairey. One, called 'Scheme B', had a swept wing, but the main offering, 'Scheme A', was based on the Delta 2, or rather the Fairey Delta Wing Transonic Research Aircraft (to ER.103D) as it was still called at the time. Construction of the latter had by

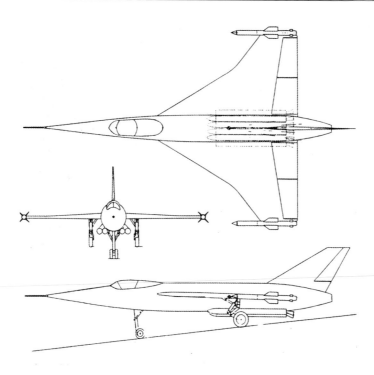

Fairey's 'Scheme A' delta-wing rocket fighter proposal to Specification F.124T was dated 23 April 1952. The drawing clearly shows the auxiliary rocket motor installation to be fitted underneath the rear fuselage. (Author's Collection)

now commenced. Fairey considered that this delta development gave the best solution to F.124T.

Maximum speed of the 'Scheme A' aircraft in level flight was given as Mach 1.3, with Mach 1.7 in a dive – these figures gave the aircraft a considerable advantage over the enemy's bombers, which at this time were expected to have a top level speed of about Mach 0.9 and up to 1.1 in a dive. This speed difference was very important when trying to make an interception, since the rocket-powered interceptor would carry only a limited amount of fuel and, as a result, have relatively short flight endurance.

Since 'Scheme A' was a direct development of the ER.103D, it would benefit from the latter's design, wind tunnel research and flight test data, and that would automatically reduce the time needed to reach first flight. The main weaponry was two Blue Jay missiles (F.124T actually called for four), and there was provision to carry wingtip-mounted containers each housing 26 rockets.

'Scheme A' would be built mostly in semi-monocoque light alloy, with much of the structure in the wing and fuselage near identical to the Delta 2. The rocket fighter did, however, introduce a cranked delta wing, with an extended chord at the tips to carry the weapons. Wing sweep was 60 degrees at the leading edge, and the thickness/chord ratio was four per cent, although this would increase locally at the tips to six per cent. The powerplant would be an 8,000lb thrust de Havilland Spectre rocket motor housed within the fuselage that used kerosene fuel, with hydrogen peroxide as the oxidant. There was also provision for six external booster rockets firing in pairs to provide a more rapid climb.

An artist's impression of Fairey's delta rocket fighter, again taken from the project brochure and showing 'Scheme A' carrying Blue Jay (Firestreak) air-to-air missiles on its wingtips. (Author's Collection)

'Scheme A's' span was 29ft 10in. with its missiles, or 27ft 6in. clean, length was 52ft 8in. with a pitot, wing area was 387sq ft and maximum take-off weight was 22,830lb. Maximum flight time was estimated to be about 15 minutes, with 3.28 minutes taken to get to 60,000ft. Both of Fairey's rocket fighter designs were rejected, and the only aircraft to fly as a result of F.124T was the Saunders-Roe SR.53, which did not progress beyond prototype status.

LONG-RANGE INTERCEPTOR

The next requirement to tempt Fairey into designing an interceptor was Specification F.155T, which was issued in January 1955, exactly three years after F.124T. This called for a two-seat day-night high-altitude fighter – in reality a highly advanced long-range all-weather interceptor. Once again Fairey offered two designs, and both were based to varying degrees on the Delta 2, but the second was a very large aeroplane.

By the time F.155T came along, the performance of enemy bomber aircraft had improved markedly over what had been possible in 1952. F.155T was a complex requirement, but it essentially described a weapon system where the aircraft and its weapon and radar were treated as a single entity (what was termed the 'weapon system concept'). The interceptor's mission was to destroy very-high-altitude enemy raiders flying in at Mach 1.3 and 60,000ft. The new aircraft would carry guided weapons only (the huge Vickers Red Dean air-to-air missile), plus the advanced AI.18 intercept radar that offered both collision course and pursuit types of attack. It was to be capable of at least Mach 2, and the minimum ceiling when flying at Mach 1.5 was given as 65,000ft. Six companies submitted designs.

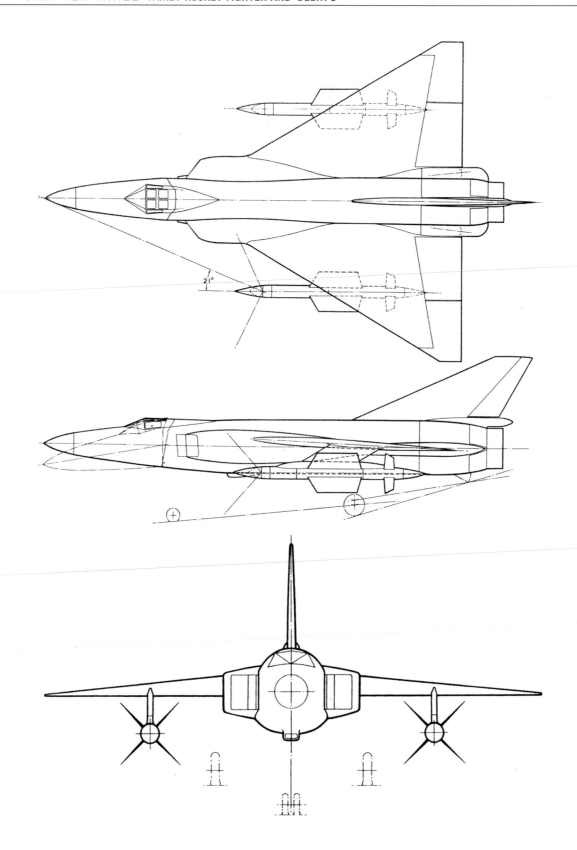

Fairey concluded that the weapon system was unlikely to be fully developed by the required date of 1962, so, alongside its very substantial main proposal, it suggested an alternative, simpler aircraft based around the Delta 2. This would have the performance to meet the threat, but could be available by 1960 or even earlier. Its powerplant was a single reheated de Havilland Gyron jet engine, with an additional Spectre rocket motor positioned on either side of an area-ruled fuselage. Like the Delta 2, the new aircraft's complete cockpit and nose section would fold down for take-off and landing, and a Blue Jay Mk 4 missile would be carried on each wingtip. The radar was the Ferranti AI.23, and the estimated performance figures indicated that Mach 2.5 could only be reached at 59,000ft using reheat. This 'modest' aircraft's span with missiles aboard was 37ft 7in., its length was 56ft 3in., gross wing area was 600sq ft, and maximum weight was 30,100lb. Service ceiling was 67,000ft.

Fairey's much larger main design proposal was to be capable of development as the full 'weapon system'. If the interceptor was built with a light alloy structure then it could meet the minimum required performance. However, to make full use of the considerable performance potential of this design and its powerplant (possibly up to Mach 3 at 36,000ft), the wing, centre fuselage and fin would in fact be built in stainless steel, while parts exposed to high temperatures would be produced in titanium. The powerplant itself was to be two Rolls-Royce RB.122 jet engines giving 19,500lb of thrust dry and 27,000lb with reheat (if necessary, the de Havilland Gyron was interchangeable with the RB.122), plus two de Havilland Spectre Junior rocket motors. The Delta 2's droop nose was retained, and it was hoped to develop this movable cabin into a self-contained jettisonable escape pod that would descend to the ground beneath a set of parachutes.

Again, Fairey considered that the experience accumulated with the construction and flight testing of both the Delta 1 and Delta 2 would carry over into this aircraft, thus saving a lot of time in the design and development process. The maximum level speed with reheat at this early stage would be Mach 2.27 at 36,000ft, although this figure would fall to Mach 1.57 if the interceptor was carrying Red Dean missiles. Maximum ceiling was 70,000ft. Span was 46ft 10in., length was 74ft 4in., gross wing area was 1,100sq ft, and maximum weight carrying Blue Jay missiles was 48,000lb, and 50,460lb with Red Deans.

The large Fairey design and the submission from Armstrong Whitworth (a project called the AW.169) were considered to be the best proposals, and in April 1956 work on both (wind tunnel testing, etc.) was permitted to continue for about another year, the AW.169 serving as a back-up to Fairey's project. At Fairey the large design was dubbed 'Delta 3', and on 25 October 1956 a model of this interceptor was successfully fired for the first time on the Larkhill test range, a speed of between Mach 1.4 and 1.8 being recorded.

In November 1956 the AW.169 was cancelled, and from this point the 'Delta 3' was looked upon as the Air Ministry requirement.

OPPOSITE
This drawing shows Fairey's smaller submission to Specification F.155T, dated October 1955. As proposed, this design carried two Blue Jay Mk 4 missiles, one on each wingtip. After the aircraft had been rejected, Fairey adapted it to take two Red Hebes on underwing pylons, as seen here. With the switch from wingtip-mounted weapons, the span became 34ft 7.5in. (Author's Collection)

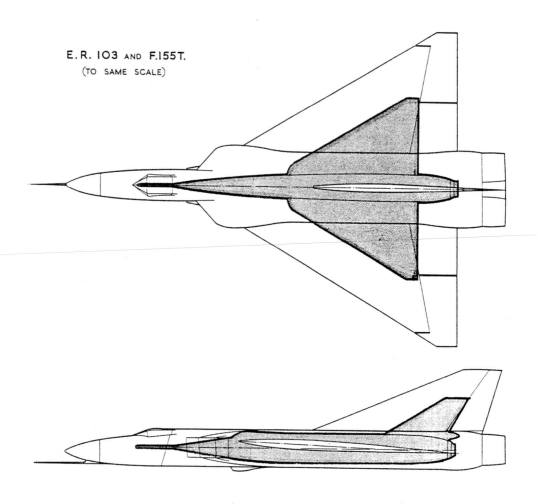

E.R. 103 AND F.155T.
(TO SAME SCALE)

However, on 4 April 1957, Minister of Defence Duncan Sandys published his famous White Paper which officially brought the abandonment of all future development of manned fighters (except for the English Electric Lightning). An order for 'Delta 3' prototypes had still to be placed, but Specification F.155 had been cancelled on 29 March, thus taking Fairey's desire to build a production jet fighter with it.

Subsequently, the company looked at adapting is massive 'Delta 3' long-range interceptor into a fighter-bomber. Along with certain changes to the airframe, the aircraft would carry a very large ventral drop tank under the rear half of the fuselage, another wing tank would go on a starboard underwing pylon, and the weapons were carried under the port wing. The latter could comprise two or four 1,000lb general purpose conventional bombs or one 'target marker' nuclear bomb. Again, these proposals were not taken up.

The extraordinary increase in size from the Delta 2 to the proposed 'Delta 3' is shown by this drawing, which is again taken from the original brochure. The Delta 3 would have been a high-speed straight-line interceptor. (Author's Collection)

OPPOSITE
In its fighter-bomber guise the 'Delta 3' design introduced changes around the air intakes and jet pipes. This view shows the aircraft 'nuclear-armed' with a 'target marker' nuclear bomb under its port wing. Note the enormous ventral fuel tank. (Author's Collection)

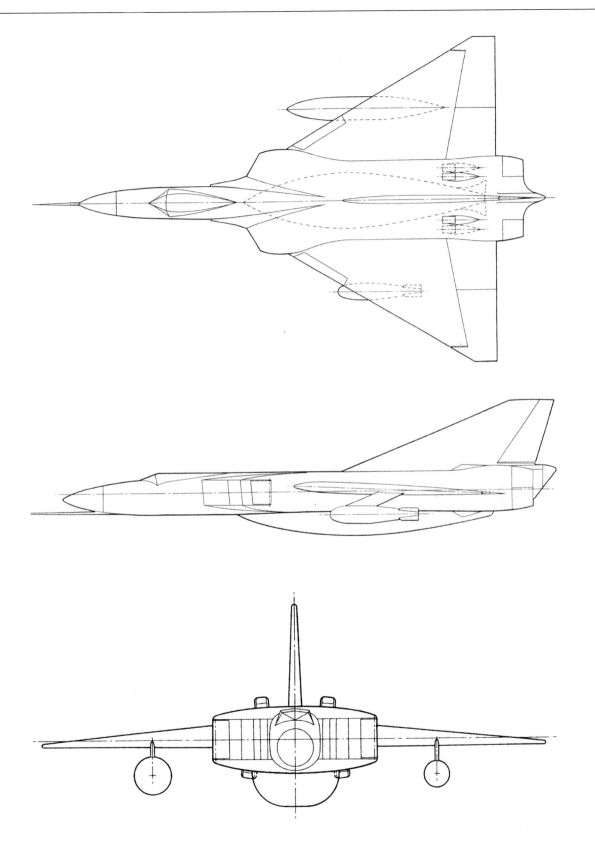

CHAPTER FOUR

CONVAIR XF-92 AND XF-92A

In August 1945 the United States Army Air Force (USAAF) issued a tentative requirement for a high-speed, high-altitude, high-performance interceptor to attack incoming enemy bombers. The winning design was the rocket-powered supersonic Model 7 project from the Consolidated Vultee Aircraft Corporation (Convair), which, on the ordering of prototypes, was designated XP-92. Following tunnel testing, the original swept-wing layout was redesigned, and by July 1946 the XP-92 had a 60-degree delta wing and a relatively short cylindrical fuselage. Problems with the airframe design, its rocket motor, plus a move of factory from Downey, in southeast Los Angeles, to San Diego in the summer of 1947 all conspired to slow the programme down, and in August 1948 the XP-92 was cancelled. Only a full-scale mock-up had been completed, which had been inspected in April 1948.

Previously, however, work on a full-size jet-powered flying scale model had started in September 1946 to evaluate the interceptor's delta wing, and this had been officially approved in January 1947. Convair called this aircraft its Model 7002 (after the project's engineering work-order number), and the USAAF allotted serial numbers 46-682 to 46-684 to three planned airframes. At first this aeroplane was officially designated XP-92A and received the name Dart but soon afterwards, when the USAAF became the US Air Force (USAF), it was retitled XF-92A because the old 'pursuit' designator had been replaced by

The sole XF-92A Dart to be built, 46-682 is pictured during roll-out at Convair's San Diego factory. Note the support structure for the raised, heavily framed, canopy, and the knife antenna directly behind the cockpit. The dark, arrowhead-shaped, strip over the nose prevented light reflections dazzling the pilot. (Gerry Balzer Collection)

RIGHT
As first built, the XF-92A had a blown frameless clear canopy, but it would never fly with this in place. Also visible in this view are the small 12AS-1000 rocket-assist take-off motors attached beneath the fuselage directly between the main undercarriage legs. (Gerry Balzer Collection)

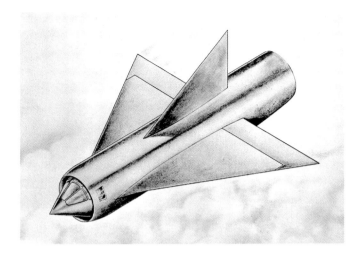

Manufacturer's impression of the Consolidated Vultee XP-92 interceptor. Although very advanced for the late 1940s, this project was ultimately cancelled in August 1948. (Gerry Balzer Collection)

F for 'fighter'. In Convair's own revised model number sequence it was subsequently redesignated Model 1.

The company's selection of the delta wing for its interceptor was aided by research uncovered in Germany after the war. In addition, Dr Alexander Lippisch, the strongest proponent of this wing in Germany, and who had now been brought to America, was consulted, and he assisted in the Dart's design. The XF-92A had initially replaced a planned XP-92 'skeleton' structural test airframe, and it would operate as a full-scale flying mock-up to assess the interceptor's aerodynamic characteristics. After the interceptor's cancellation, the XF-92A was retained for research flying to assess the delta wing's stability and control, to establish structural design criteria, and to determine the machine's performance. Serials 46-683 and 46-684 were not built.

Most of the Dart's airframe was built by the Vultee Division in Downey, with Adolph Burstein as Project Engineer. However, the company closed its Vultee Field operations in mid-1947 and moved the project to San Diego, the airframe arriving in about July when around 75 per cent complete and with just the canopy, aft fuselage, elevons and rudder to be added. Final assembly at Convair's Experimental Manufacturing Facility was completed at the end of

October 1947, and around the turn of the year Thomas M. Hemphill took over as XF-92A Project Engineer, with the airframe then complete but lacking an engine.

However, according to the USAF, the move to San Diego was a big factor in the programme falling a year behind schedule, despite the aircraft having utilised components from numerous other types to save time. For example, the engine and wheel brakes came from the Lockheed P-80 Shooting Star, the nose and main landing gear of its retractable tricycle undercarriage came from a Bell P-63 Kingcobra and a North American FJ-1 Fury, respectively, and the ejection seat from Convair's own YP-81 escort fighter prototype. Overall, the airframe was similar to the XF-92 interceptor, bar a change in where the single-seat cockpit was positioned.

In appearance, the XF-92A was characterised by its mid-fuselage position, 60-degree sweep, delta wing of low thickness/chord ratio and a large vertical fin. The wing planform was a unilateral triangle, there was no horizontal tailplane and the delta-shaped vertical tail was similar in appearance to the semi-wing (the rudder ran to nearly the full height of the fin). Of aluminium structure, the full cantilever wing used two spars and had elevons that extended along the full length of the trailing edge. The controls themselves were irreversible and 100 per cent hydraulically operated, both control column and rudder pedal forces were produced artificially by a spring system and contained a variable 'feel', and the aircraft had no other flight control surfaces such as flaps, slats or speed brakes.

The XF-92A had a short, circular fuselage and its fuselage-mounted jet engine was served by a bifurcated nose air intake and an aft exhaust which, after reheat had been installed, extended well beyond the tailplane. The internal fuel capacity came to 560 gallons, held entirely in seven bladder-type fuel cells and all located within fuselage compartments. Although designed by Convair to test the flight characteristics of a delta wing configuration for a future fighter-type aircraft (what became the F-102), the XF-92A was simply a research aircraft, and so lacked many systems and much of the equipment associated with high-performance aeroplanes.

On 4–6 November 1947, Model 7002 46-682 was taken (in secrecy) to the NACA Ames research facility at Moffett Field, California, aboard the attack cargo ship USS *Titania* (AKA-13) to undergo full-scale testing in a low-speed wind tunnel. Between 2 and 23 December no

Parked next to the seaplane ramp at Consolidated Vultee's San Diego plant, the XF-92A has its engine run up in this official company photograph. The inside of the air intake is painted red. (Terry Panopalis Collection)

fewer than 96 trials were undertaken that provided results confirming previous scale-model wind-tunnel data. The airframe was then shipped back to San Diego in January 1948 aboard the carrier USS *Boxer* (CV-21) to have its powerplant fitted. Initially this was to be a 4,600lb thrust Allison J33-A-21 turbojet which, at such a low power rating, was used only for taxi tests. If it had indeed been used for flight, the turbojet would have placed too high a load on the aircraft's 12AS-1000 rocket-assisted motors on take-off.

Next, on 26 March 1948, 46-682 was taken aboard the tank landing ship USS *Hillsborough County* (LST-827) on the first leg of its journey to Muroc Air Force Base (AFB), California, where it arrived by road on 31 March. Muroc was home to many of the USAF's experimental test programmes, and in June 1951 it would become the USAF Flight Test Center. Reassembly began on 5 April, and a prolonged spell of ground testing and taxi runs followed. The designated XF-92A project pilot was Convair Chief of Flight Research Ellis D. 'Sam' Shannon, who performed the first taxi at Muroc on 25 May. On 9 June, having realised that the aircraft's lateral control was too sensitive, and becoming airborne would help him to stabilise this, Shannon took 46-682 on a two mile-long 'hop' just 15ft above the ground.

A flight-cleared Allison J33-A-23 engine from the proposed, but unbuilt, F-80D, fitted with a new exhaust pipe and modified tail cone, was installed in early September 1948. This provided 5,200lb of thrust (with water injection for thrust augmentation) and gave a gross take-off weight of 12,552lb. In addition, 46-682 had its original bubble canopy replaced by a high-speed canopy and windshield.

At last, on 18 September 1948, Shannon took the XF-92A Dart on an 18-minute maiden flight, thus making it the first delta wing aircraft to fly anywhere. This also began what was termed Phase I testing. The pilot found that the aircraft was certainly underpowered, and also that the control system was 'extremely sensitive to minute control stick deflections'. Nevertheless, by February 1949 a total of 19 flights had been logged, although 46-682's lack of engine power was evidenced by an excessive take-off run. All 47 Phase I flights were conducted by Convair pilots Sam Shannon and Bill Martin, the latter having made his first flight in the XF-92A on 6 January 1949. From then on he and Shannon shared the flying.

February 1949 also saw the start of a detailed evaluation of 46-682's behaviour during take-off, when climbing, in the cruise, and, finally, landing. One problem uncovered by Martin was a loud buzz encountered at Mach 0.75, which was found to come from a loose VHF knife antenna immediately to the rear of the pilot's canopy, and thus easily rectified. Cut-off elevons were also tested on a few flights, but the original full-span elevons were soon refitted. Low-speed testing was completed in early August, and from 10 August 1949 the pilots began to dive the aircraft to transonic speeds. After gradually increasing the speed on each dive, a figure of Mach 0.925 was eventually recorded.

Manufacturer's Phase I flying was concluded on 26 August 1949 after 47 flights. The aircraft had actually been formally accepted by

CONVAIR XF-92A DART

XF-92A 46-682 is depicted here in its original configuration,
prior to the installation of an afterburner.

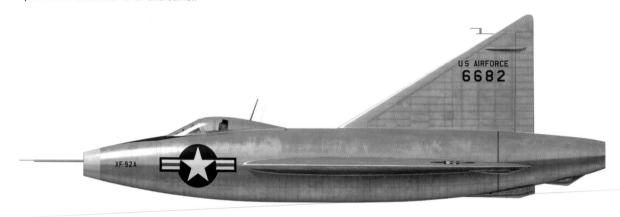

the USAF three months earlier, on 14 May, when it had completed
30 flights, and despite some Phase I work still needing to be finished
by Convair.

Capt Charles E. 'Chuck' Yeager began the USAF trials programme
(Phase II testing) on 13 October 1949. This was his first flight in
the aeroplane, and in it he performed the first barrel rolls ever made
by the XF-92A. Phase II would embrace 25 flights, and include an
evaluation of the delta wing's stability and control characteristics.
From late November Yeager shared the flying with Maj Frank K. 'Pete'
Everest, who made his initial flight in 46-682 on the 23rd of that
month. From then on, during Phase II, one of these pilots would fly
the delta while the other would fly chase, and as such they expanded
the flight envelope and assessed the aircraft's behaviour in level flight,
in dives and in rolls.

On one occasion Everest pointed the XF-92A's nose directly
down in a dive from height and, using maximum engine thrust,
managed to reach supersonic speed, but he was barely able to get
the aircraft to pass through the sound barrier. There was no other
way of achieving Mach 1 with 46-682 because of its lack of engine
power. Everest reported, however, 'we found that the delta planform
handled very well during the transition from subsonic to supersonic
speeds, in comparison with the straight-wing [Lockheed] F-94 and
the swept wing [North American] F-86, which encountered severe
buffeting and loss of control effectiveness in this speed region'.
Phase II testing ended on 28 December 1949. Figures recorded
during this period, at an engine start weight of 13,500lb, included
a maximum level flight Mach number of 0.85 at 21,000ft, a rate of
climb (using water-alcohol injection) of 5,250ft per minute, a time
to 35,000ft of 20.6 minutes and an absolute ceiling of 40,000ft.

In early January 1950, several other USAF pilots, including Cols Albert
Boyd and Fred Ascani, flew 46-682 to enable them to experience flight

X PLANES
CONVAIR XF-92A DART

in a delta-winged aeroplane. At transonic speed, the XF-92A proved to be very stable, and it was quite easy to manoeuvre and to land. However, pilots found that they could not put it into a spin. It also proved difficult to stall because, unlike a conventional-winged aeroplane, 46-682 would not produce an abrupt nose pitch down with the wing in a stalled condition, but rather would sink rapidly whilst still in a horizontal attitude.

With Phase II over, Capt Yeager had intended to fly the aircraft back to the Convair plant in San Diego on 12 May, but the engine failed at a height of just 20ft shortly after take-off. The subsequent emergency landing on the dry lake without the benefit of landing gear, because there was no time to deploy it, caused serious damage. The Dart was sent to Convair for repairs to be made to its badly damaged airframe. The company also took this opportunity to modify the XF-92A. It would be 14 months before the jet aircraft flew again.

The lack of engine thrust was addressed by the fitting of a new engine, an Allison J33-A-29, which introduced an afterburner. The unit gave 5,600lb of thrust dry and 7,500lb with reheat, and it was hoped that

The Dart is seen here back at Edwards after being upgraded with an afterburning Allison J33 engine in early 1951. The aircraft's small air intake would prove a problem for the reheated versions of the powerplant fitted from now on. (Gerry Balzer Collection)

this would increase the maximum Mach number attainable. This installation also necessitated major airframe modifications, in particular a rear fuselage extension to house the afterburner inside a longer, more cylindrical tail cone. The XF-92A's bare metal finish was also now hidden beneath a all-white livery to help observers with optical tracking in flight. The aircraft's gross take-off weight had risen to 14,398lb.

Back again at Edwards AFB (as Muroc had been renamed in December 1949), Yeager flew the XF-92A's first sortie with the new engine on 20 July 1951. This opened a detailed assessment of 46-682's performance with an afterburning powerplant, but the results overall were poor because the afterburner would continually flame out at heights above 38,000ft. The tail cone would also overheat, and 46-682 spent long periods on the ground undergoing maintenance and refits. Overall, there was little significant gain in performance over the old J33-A-23 unit. Although higher subsonic speeds were recorded, the service ceiling was still around 37,000ft, and not the 40,000ft or even 50,000ft hoped for by Convair. The new engine also proved less reliable, while dive recoveries from Mach 1 now included buffeting and porpoising.

In this second set of USAF trials Everest and Yeager between them accumulated a further 21 flights in all, the last on 6 February 1953, before the USAF handed the aircraft over to NACA to conduct its own research programme.

This lack of thrust was partly due to the fact that the engine inlet duct, because of its length and sensitivity to mass flow and AoA, functioned poorly. Flight trials had shown that the rate of climb was good up to 35,000–37,000ft, but then dropped off markedly above this altitude. Also, the true airspeed fell away rapidly at heights below 10,000ft. In addition, the Dart's dive and high-speed flight investigations had been restricted because of the aircraft's inability to enter dives at altitudes of no higher than 38,000–40,000ft. A maximum true Mach number of 1.01 was obtained after diving for 7,000ft from an altitude of around 38,400ft, but it was considered that much higher Mach numbers could have been recorded if it had been possible to enter dives at around 45,000ft.

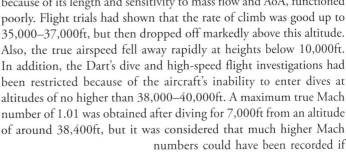

46-682 was photographed in April 1953 with tufting attached to the starboard wing and rear fuselage. Except for the outer part of the starboard elevon, the elevons and rudder have either been painted grey or left unpainted. (Gerry Balzer Collection)

NACA TRIALS

In 1953 the sole XF-92A went back to San Diego to have yet another new engine installed – a J33-A-16 which provided 8,600lb of reheated thrust. It was then transferred to NACA for a planned series of 30 flights to provide further knowledge for future supersonic aircraft. The project pilot for this new programme was Scott Crossfield of NACA's High-Speed Flight Research Station at Edwards (which later became NASA's Flight Research Center). For its

new operator, 46-682 was fitted
with a considerable volume of
recording equipment.

On 9 April 1953, Crossfield
flew the first of 25 flights he
would make in the XF-92A,
and he found the aeroplane was
still very sensitive to control
motions. His next flight was
made with tufting attached to the
starboard wing and rear fuselage
and, when making windup turns
(which sees the aircraft entering
into a banked turn at constant
altitude and constant Mach and
with increasing normal acceleration or AoA – i.e. the radius
of the turn is slowly decreased) to photograph these tufts,
he experienced a very strong pitch-up and pitch down at
Mach 0.87 at 29,000ft. During the flight programme this pitch-up
often exceeded 6g, and on one occasion 8g, although after this second
flight the NACA programme was conducted at lower altitudes.

Towards the end of June 46-682 had fences added to its wings at
60 per cent semi span. It was intended to fit these to Convair's F-102
interceptor, and on the Dart they stretched from the leading edge to
the elevon junction. The plan was to perform ten flights to see if these
wing fences could reduce the aircraft's tendency to pitch up at low
speeds and in turns. Crossfield undertook the first flight with fences in
place (NACA Flight 14) on 3 July 1953, and the first six were made at
under Mach 1 and the remaining four at low speeds. During one sortie
the fences buckled. Nevertheless, it was clear that they had produced
an overall improvement in the XF-92's stability characteristics, and the
fences had also held back the onset of pitch-up and reduced its force at
low and medium Mach numbers, but unfortunately not at high Mach
numbers – here, the pitch-up was still severe.

Such was the improvement that in mid-July NACA added fences
along the wing underside at around 20 per cent local wing chord.
On 22 July, when Crossfield first flew 46-682 with these additions,
he found that the aircraft's stability and control characteristics up to
Mach 0.8 were now even better. He was also pleased to report that its
low-speed lateral-directional control characteristics had been improved
too. Further flights, however, showed that the aircraft's behaviour above
Mach 0.8 was still no better.

A report dated 26 May 1955, which looked at all of NACA's flying,
recorded that 'the investigation included sideslips, aileron rolls, and
rudder pulses at altitudes ranging from 18,000ft to 30,000ft at indicated
speeds from 160mph to 420mph'. Having wing fences installed at
60 per cent of the wing semi span had provided a comparison to the
'basic airplane'.

All of the pilots who flew the Dart (during the earlier joint NACA–
USAF trials and the current NACA programme) had objected to the

Late in its career the XF-92A flew with fences fitted to the upper wing and then to the wing underside as well. This appears to be the only known photograph of the aircraft with fences in place, and is in fact a cropped version of a well-known view showing seven different NACA High-Speed Flight Research Station aircraft. It appears that both upper and lower wing fences are in place here – if indeed so, then this dates the photograph as mid-July 1953 onwards. (NASA)

aircraft's overall lateral handling characteristics, particularly at low speeds, primarily because of the high roll-to-sideslip ratios. These adverse characteristics had been aggravated at low speeds by high adverse yaw and rough air, and at high speeds by excessive aircraft response to small control deflections. The lateral handling characteristics at low speeds had been improved by the installation of the wing fences – an improvement which appeared to result from an increase in the aircraft's static directional stability.

The NACA report concluded that 'the capabilities of the delta wing were still limited by insufficient power'. With the power available (at a take-off weight of 15,500lb), maximum speeds of Mach 0.922 (707mph) at 15,000ft and Mach 0.94 (721mph) at 35,000ft had been achieved. The sea level rate of climb was 8,850ft per minute, and the absolute ceiling was 41,000ft.

RETIREMENT

With the completion of trials with fences, the USAF asked NACA to fit a drag parachute to the Dart to provide further background research for the F-102. Taxi runs over the dry lake bed at Edwards showed that this parachute would deploy effectively without producing any adverse problems, and on 30 September 1953 Crossfield made the first flight with the drag chute installed. On 14 October 1953 Crossfield undertook two more flights in 46-682, both of which looked at low-speed lateral and directional control without the wing fences installed. The second of these proved to be the Dart's final flight.

Having landed, and after the pilot had jettisoned the drag chute, 46-682's nose began to droop whilst taxiing. The aircraft then slewed around in a hard-left turn before settling onto its nose, starboard landing gear and starboard wingtip. On inspection it was found that the nose strut attachment had failed, which in turn had made the

After a flight made on 14 October 1953 (with the wing fences now removed), part of the Dart's nose undercarriage leg failed, which put the aircraft in this unfortunate position and brought a close to its flying career. Legendary test pilot Scott Crossfield was at the controls at the time, and he later commented 'Nobody wanted to fly the XF-92. There was no line-up of pilots for that airplane. It was a miserable flying beast. Everyone complained it was underpowered.' Crossfield had flown the Dart 25 times prior to this career-ending accident. (Gerry Balzer Collection)

shock strut buckle and fold up (which caused the aircraft to slew). The damage could be repaired but the value of what was now quite an elderly aeroplane made the cost prohibitive, and so 46-682 was grounded and retired. More modern aircraft were becoming available – indeed, one of the F-102 prototypes had already been assigned to the High-Speed Flight Research Station.

As an aside, earlier in its career the Dart had been painted in a new livery to enable it to represent a Soviet 'MiG-23' fighter. This was for the feature film *Jet Pilot* shot in the early 1950s, although in the end the footage taken of the aircraft was not included in the movie (the XF-92A did, however, appear in another film called *Toward the Unknown*, released in 1956).

In late 1951 some thought had been given to rebuilding 46-682 as a flying prototype for the F-102 interceptor, but the engineering task and the cost were clearly just not worth the effort. Also, an XF-92A interceptor version had been proposed to the US Navy in September 1948, but this was rejected.

In all, Model 7002 XF-92A Dart 46-682 accumulated 118 flights in its career for a total flying time of approximately 62 hours. It achieved a maximum speed in a dive of Mach 1.1, and with its more powerful engines the service ceiling was 40,000ft and absolute ceiling 41,000ft. The XF-92A's span was 31ft 4in., length with the extended jet pipe was 42ft 9.6in, wing area was 425sq ft and the vertical fin area 59.9sq ft.

Convair's XF-92A should really have received a designation in the USAF's experimental X-plane series. Nevertheless, in a varied flying career, it validated the concept of a thin delta wing and provided substantial data and support for the development of the F-102 Delta Dagger, for Convair's other delta wing projects that followed (the F-106 Delta Dart, B-58 Hustler bomber and F2Y Sea Dart), and for the American aircraft industry in general. The XF-92A showed that a delta-winged aeroplane was a practical idea for transonic and supersonic flight, but with a shortage of engine thrust and severe pitch-up problems, the aircraft itself was flawed. Convair found that the maximum lift coefficient of the XF-92A's wing was not high, and was obtained at very high AoA only. Otherwise, the delta wing had performed admirably, and was clearly a good basis on which to produce a supersonic interceptor.

On retirement, 46-682 was donated by the USAF to the University of the South at Sewanee, in Tennessee. In August 1969 it was transferred to the USAF Museum at Wright-Patterson AFB, Ohio, which is where it resides today, fully restored in its white livery, with the inside of the nose intake painted red. The XF-92A has to be one of the unsung heroes of the worldwide 1950s research effort to produce supersonic aeroplanes.

The Dart painted up as the fictional 'MiG-23' for the film *Jet Pilot*, starring John Wayne and Janet Leigh. The colour scheme was quite complex with a black-green and sky blue mix, plus red lettering that was lined in white. Note that the starboard wingtip has been left unpainted. The short and narrow jet pipe shows that filming took place before the aeroplane had an afterburning engine installed. Sadly, footage of the aircraft was not included in the motion picture upon its release to the public in November 1957 – almost eight years after the 'MiG-23' had been filmed. (Author's Collection)

CHAPTER FIVE

CONVAIR F-102 AND F-106

Early YF-102 53-1785 was photographed on the ramp at Edwards in 1955 whilst flying with the NACA High-Speed Flight Station. This view provides good detail for the heavily framed cockpit canopy, air intake and the long tube-like fuselage that had no area-ruling. As such, it could not go supersonic in level flight. The aircraft also experienced severe pitch-up characteristics when manoeuvring, and to counter this NACA fitted fences to the outer section of the wings – clearly visible here. (NASA)

When comparing the Fairey and Convair delta-winged aircraft programmes, the Delta I and XF-92A seemed to have had much in common. Both were relatively straightforward research machines designed to sample the qualities of the delta wing, and both were subsonic in level flight. Each manufacturer then moved on to larger designs – the Delta 2 and the F-102 described here, although Convair's product was bigger and heavier than Fairey's machine. The American type would enjoy a prolonged production run and was developed into even more capable versions, while the Delta 2 remained a prototype. However, the F-102 experienced considerable development problems.

SPECIFICATION MX-1554

Prompted by a growing threat to the US mainland from attack by Soviet bombers, the USAF opened a competition for a new supersonic single-seat near-all-weather interceptor called the '1954 Interceptor' (the planned service entry date) in January 1949. Specification MX-1554 was raised to cover the aircraft, which stated an armament of Hughes Falcon air-to-air missiles and 2.75in. folding-fin aircraft rockets only, speeds well in excess of Mach 1 at heights in excess of 50,000ft, and a combat ceiling of 60,000ft.

The aircraft's electronics and fire control system (FCS), also supplied by Hughes, were covered by Specification MX-1179, and the interceptor was to be produced as a weapon system – i.e. the airframe would be designed around its (increasingly complex) equipment rather than having items brought in separately to be installed inside an existing structure.

Convair's proposal was selected as the clear winner, and in due course it was designated F-102 and named Delta Dagger – Convair knew the aircraft as the Model 8. Flight experience with the XF-92A (Model 7002) and wind tunnel tests had indicated that a 60-degree delta configuration would meet or exceed all of the requirements. The choice was a four per cent thick delta wing swept 60 degrees at the leading edge, and with no flaps, leading-edge slats or horizontal tail, longitudinal and lateral control came from elevons on the wing's trailing edge. A triangular vertical tail with a conventional rudder was also chosen, and the armament (six Falcons or 24 rockets in the final F-102A) would go in two bays placed underneath the engine. Apart from a longer, solid and pointed nose to house the radar and the resulting side air intakes, the new design was basically an outgrowth of the XF-92A. However, the lateral intakes produced a different appearance and the airframe had been largely redesigned.

Convair decided to use an exceptionally high proportion of heavy-press forged components in the F-102 airframe so that complete fuselage frames, wing spars and longitudinal members could all be produced from single large forgings. It was estimated that this move reduced the weight of each aircraft by more than 100lb and saved 273 components and 3,200 rivets.

The production run would also follow (for the first time) what was called the Cook-Craigie Plan. Gens Orval Cook and Laurence Craigie had created an 'ideal' production plan, which at first would see a limited production rate to allow faults in the design to be eliminated by flight trials, after which the rate would be accelerated. The generals believed that an intensive flight-testing programme, using an increasing number of completed airframes, should uncover and solve all of the aircraft's major problems and weaknesses in much quicker time than had traditionally been the case using a small number of prototypes. By adopting the plan, the USAF hoped that all technical issues would be ironed out well before the production run reached its maximum rate.

However, by December 1951, it seemed probable that the Model 8's Wright J67 engine and Hughes MX-1179 radar would be late, and that the 1954 in-service date would be missed. Consequently, the USAF

This Convair model depicts the company's original proposal to Specification MX-1554 from early 1951. (Author's Collection)

told Convair to proceed with an already proposed 'interim' interceptor fitted with a 'current' Westinghouse J40 engine and a less capable FCS (for a while this was called the F-102A, before reverting to just F-102). The later 'ultimate' version (using the same airframe, but fitted with the J67 and MX-1179 FCS) would now become the F-102B. The interim version could destroy the types of enemy bombers anticipated prior to 1954, while the 'ultimate' aircraft would deal with potential supersonic bombers expected after 1954.

The interim interceptor, however, began to experience problems of its own. Firstly, continuous increases in weight meant that the J40 could no longer provide the requisite speed and altitude performance, so it was replaced by a Pratt & Whitney J57-P-11 giving 9,200lb of thrust on dry power and 14,800lb with afterburner. Next, NACA wind tunnel data indicated that the estimated maximum altitude (57,000ft) and combat radius (350 miles) were overly optimistic because the aircraft's bulky rear fuselage and wing created far too much drag. In fact, by mid-1952, both the USAF's Wright Air Development Center Aircraft Laboratory and NACA had become unhappy with Convair's 'low' drag estimates, although the manufacturer itself did not concur. In October NACA was asked to evaluate a 1/20th scale high-speed wind tunnel model of the F-102, and in February 1953 it confirmed that Convair's estimates were significantly different from its own data.

In mid-1953 Convair finally accepted that its original design was in error, and that the fuselage needed to be reshaped so that it conformed to the new theory of 'area rule'. The concept that 'interference drag at transonic speed depended almost entirely on the distribution of the aircraft's total cross-sectional area along the direction of flight' had been verified in December 1952 by aerodynamicist Richard T. Whitcomb and his team using new transonic wind tunnels in the NACA Langley Laboratory, in Virginia.

In practice, to apply area rule meant that any additions to cross-sectional area (for example the engine nacelles or wings) had to be compensated by subtractions from the area elsewhere (for example by narrowing the adjacent parts of the fuselage). This simple empirical law, if applied properly to an aircraft's design, would result in minimum transonic and supersonic drag, particularly at speeds between Mach 0.75 and 1.2. In fact, transonic drag would be reduced substantially. As designed, Convair's F-102 did not conform to this rule.

As a result, on 28 August 1953 (still before first flight) Convair proposed the following changes to the airframe to reduce the drag problem:

1. The addition of cambered leading edges and reflexed (upturned) wingtips, the latter having the camber line curving back up near the trailing edge.
2. Moving the wings rearwards and having the vertical fin in a new position.
3. An extension to the fuselage length of some seven feet.
4. Re-working the fuselage into an 'area-rule' or 'coke-bottle' shape.
5. Moving some of the aircraft's internal components.

This new design was tested in the wind tunnel during April

1954, but it continued to show a deficiency in performance, with the estimated maximum speed now Mach 1.01, and not Mach 1.32 as first forecast. Furthermore, these airframe and component changes had increased the aircraft's weight by some 3,500lb.

SUBSONIC INTERCEPTOR

The Cook-Craigie plan made no accommodation for true prototypes, so the first ten F-102s ordered were designated YF-102 pre-production airframes. Having been taken to Edwards AFB by road, the first of these non-area-ruled YF-102s (52-7994) made its maiden flight on 24 October 1953 with Convair test pilot Richard L. 'Dick' Johnson at the controls. On 2 November, however, the aircraft crashed on the runway at the start of its seventh flight after a fuel system problem made the engine flame-out on take-off. Johnson suffered serious injuries (he returned to the flight programme in April 1954) and the airframe was damaged beyond repair.

Flying resumed on 11 January 1954 when the second YF-102 (52-7995) first became airborne, flown by Sam Shannon. The programme proceeded normally until higher speed trials uncovered severe buffeting at Mach 0.9 and, as foretold by the wind tunnel, Mach 1 proved out of reach in level flight. In fact, the interceptor in this original form was drag-limited in level flight to Mach 0.98 and its ceiling was just 48,000ft (with some difficulty, it did reach Mach 1.06 in a dive). Maj Gen Albert Boyd became the first USAF pilot to fly 52-7995 with a sortie on 28 April 1954.

The first YF-102, 52-7994, had a predominantly all-metal finish. This aircraft crashed following engine failure and was damaged beyond repair just nine days after its first flight. (Terry Panopalis Collection)

Undercarriage problems were quite common during the F-102 test phases, with the hydraulic pistons in the landing gear actuators often being to blame. With his aircraft possibly suffering from just such an issue, the pilot of F-102A-15-CO of the Air Research and Development Command chose to take the runway barrier (possibly at Edwards AFB). The jet's right main landing gear collapsed during the course of the landing. 53-1800 retains the small vertical stabiliser and early speed-brake configuration. (USAF)

Convair had a subsonic aeroplane on its hands, and this threatened the future of the entire programme. In its original form, the YF-102 had not been a particularly inspired design, and its mediocre performance gave sufficient grounds for cancellation. Somehow the drag had to be drastically reduced, and Convair began work on another major redesign, which involved the following:

1. A further extension of the fuselage by four feet to increase the length-to-diameter 'fineness ratio', plus a 'sharpened' nose.

2. A new lighter canopy with a modified windscreen, a narrower hood and flat side-panels. Also moved slightly forward, it gave an improved airflow and an improved pilot view (vision out of the YF-102 when flying at extreme AoA had proved inadequate).

3. A new fairing around an enlarged rear fuselage. The area rule did not necessarily require a fuselage to be narrowed for it to work properly – additions could in fact be made, so bulged streamlined areas were introduced that extended beyond the exhaust to delay flow breakaway. This revision of the fuselage profile reduced the cross-sectional area over the wing, while the large bulged fillets and filling-in flanking the jet pipe and propelling nozzle prevented a sudden increase in cross-sectional area.

4. The wings were given partial 'conical camber' – a progressive increase in leading-edge camber from the root to near the tip. This reduced drag at high altitudes and improved the aircraft's behaviour at high AoA.

5. Revised, cut back, engine intake ducts.

6. A more powerful J57-P-23 engine, producing 10,200lb of thrust dry and 16,000lb with afterburner, rather more than the J57-P-11 giving 9,200lb of thrust dry and 14,800lb with afterburner.

7. A substantial reduction in weight, helped significantly by a lighter engine support structure. Looking at the detail design more closely, Convair also improved accessibility to the interior equipment, some of which had previously needed the removal of the complete powerplant when maintenance was required.

This new design was officially designated F-102A in May 1954 – the second time the designation had been used. These major modifications wreaked havoc with the Cook-Craigie plan, and its timetable, an element of which was the acquisition of production tooling at an early stage in the aircraft's development. By October 1953 Convair had purchased 30,000 tools for the production line, but 20,000 of these now had to be discarded and replaced by new tooling. The F-102 programme had exposed the weaknesses in the Cook-Craigie theories, but the modified airframe was also now very different to the 'ultimate' F-102B and could no longer use that aircraft's powerplant or FCS.

The ten YF-102 airframes embraced the first two flight articles and a further eight built to the original configuration. Four more manufactured to the first major redesign configuration were also called YF-102s, and these latter machines were used entirely for flight trials and never modified. The YF-102s essentially became research aircraft, and later in its career, for trials purposes, 52-7995 had a new nose attached in the form to be used by the supersonic YF-102A detailed below. However, this was the only change, the aircraft retaining its non-area-ruled fuselage and braced canopy.

SUPERSONIC INTERCEPTOR

In November 1954 the USAF issued a set of general operational requirements for the F-102A, requesting Mach 1.23 at 35,000ft and a good altitude performance up to 54,000ft (a structural limitation would keep the maximum speed to Mach 1.5). The first non-area-ruled production F-102, 53-1787 and designated YF-102A, was modified 'synthetically' to the upgraded configuration, with fillets designed to represent the new shapes attached over parts of the basic airframe. A J57-P-23 was installed, and the aircraft was nicknamed 'Hot Rod' because of its estimated higher speed and also for the pace at which the modifications had been completed by Convair – just 117 working days from the start of the redesign. 53-1787 made its maiden flight,

The first YF-102A prototype was 53-1787, seen here. The aircraft presents a much sleeker profile compared to the original YF-102s and, with so many differences in design, the two aircraft were as chalk is to cheese. (Gerald Balzer Collection)

The substantial fairings positioned on either side of the rear fuselage and jet pipe to complete the area-ruling of the YF-102A's fuselage are clearly shown in this air-to-air photograph of highly polished Delta Dagger 56-1041. (Gerald Balzer Collection)

from Lindbergh Field, in San Diego, on 20 December 1954, and the next day it reached Mach 1.2 at 35,000ft with ease. In fact, pilot Dick Johnson was able to go supersonic during the climb. The take-off run had also been reduced.

53-1787 was one of four service test aircraft (the others were 53-1788, -1789 and -1790), and the next jet, 53-1788, retained the heavily braced canopy used by the original YF-102s (the other three had new canopies). Phase I performance testing was held between 20 December 1954 and the end of February 1955, and, on 21 January 1955, 53-1787 recorded an altitude of 55,130ft – the highest so far. Early flight trials by USAF pilots showed that stability needed improvement, but overall the aircraft flew well.

The first production F-102A built to the lightweight area-ruled configuration made its maiden flight at Edwards on 24 June 1955 and was accepted by the USAF five days later. F-102A clearance flying eventually involved nearly 50 aircraft, including the original YF-102s, at several Air Force bases. One major change subsequently made to the aircraft would be the fitting of a larger fin to deal with a previously unknown phenomenon called 'inertia coupling' or 'roll coupling'. This affected new high-performance aircraft, with long fuselages and short wings, when flying supersonically. During roll manoeuvres, it would make the airframe diverge viciously in pitch and yaw. The F-102A's fin area was duly increased from 68.8sq ft to 94sq ft and the height raised by 2ft 9in. The 23rd production machine, 53-1813, took the new fin on its first flight on 10 December 1955, and it was introduced to the production line in 1956 on airframe 66 – earlier examples were retrofitted. This feature also improved the F-102A's manoeuvrability for certain roles.

At this stage, however, the F-102A's performance still fell short of that desired by the USAF, and in 1955 the first example received yet more alterations to its air intakes. As modified, the aircraft was able to reach Mach 1.5, and on 18 January 1956 it recorded Mach 1.535. In the meantime, the Phase II trials programme involving the early YF-102As – primarily an evaluation of their stability and control and their flying qualities in general – came to an end in March 1956. Afterwards, the first YF-102A had a new jet pipe shape fitted to represent that used by the F-106A. The flight assessment of this jet pipe lasted until 25 April 1956.

F-106 DELTA DART

In June 1956 the F-102B 'ultimate' interceptor, having undergone engineering changes that had turned it into a new aircraft, was redesignated F-106 and named Delta Dart. This programme would also experience problems, but whereas the F-102's had centred on the airframe and aerodynamics, the F-106 was held back by technical difficulties. This in turn resulted in planned orders for the jet being cut back because of funding issues.

It was mid-1954 before the MX-1179 FCS could be installed in a testbed airframe for trials, and by August 1953 the Wright J67 was running nearly a year late – both factors that delayed the interceptor's service entry. The engine was an Americanised version of the Bristol Olympus, but its development became protracted and in 1955 the USAF finally abandoned plans to put it into production. It was replaced in the F-102B (F-106) by the Pratt & Whitney J75, a move approved early in 1955.

The J75-P-17 installed in the F-106A gave 17,200lb of thrust dry and 24,500lb with reheat, and contributed to a much higher speed over the Delta Dagger. Aside from superior engine performance, the 'ultimate' Convair interceptor was to have much greater capability overall than the F-102. It was to be armed with guided missiles fitted with conventional or atomic warheads and would be capable of intercepting enemy aircraft under all weather conditions at heights approaching 70,000ft (later 55,000ft) and at speeds up to Mach 2 at 35,000ft. These interceptions would be made under automatic guidance from the ground and/or from the interceptor's radar.

The first of two prototype F-106s completed its maiden flight on 26 December 1956. USAF test flying subsequently commenced on 29 April 1957 from Edwards, and initially looked encouraging when Mach 1.9 and an altitude of 57,000ft were recorded. But Category II testing completed in 1957 revealed that both the acceleration and top

RIGHT
The F-106 was not the end of Convair's delta wing interceptor studies. This company model for a developed Delta Dart has canard foreplanes and box-shaped air intakes, and it is thought to date possibly from the late 1950s. The area-ruled fuselage is well shown. (Author's Collection)

56-0451, the very first Delta Dart, was ordered as an F-102B, but on 17 June 1956 it was redesignated F-106A. On 14 December the aircraft was taken by land from its Convair San Diego birthplace to the Air Force Flight Test Center at Edwards for its first flights and Phase I testing. Taxi trials commenced on 22 December 1956 and the first flight followed four days later. The Delta Dart was passed on to the USAF in May 1957, at which point it officially became a YF-106A. (Gerald Balzer Collection)

A quite extraordinary view, possibly taken at Edwards AFB, showing three different Convair interceptor designs parked next to each other. The two on the left (57-0230 and 56-0466) are F-106A Delta Darts, then F-102A Delta Dagger 57-0878 and, finally, YF-102 53-1780. There is a clear family likeness throughout, but in particular note the differences in cockpit canopies and tailfins. (Gerald Balzer Collection)

speed of the two prototypes were down on the estimated figures. In fact, because of the aeroplane's poor acceleration, speeds above Mach 1.7 were essentially not useable (nearly 4.5 minutes were needed to reach Mach 1.7 from Mach 1, and then a further 2.5 minutes to take the speed up to Mach 1.8). Also in 1957, severe cash problems forced the USAF to consider cuts, and at one stage dropping the entire F-106 production run was considered. In the end the project was retained, but a much smaller number of airframes was manufactured than first planned.

The original YF-102 had a span of 37ft 0in., a length of 52ft 6in., a gross wing area of 661sq ft and a gross weight of 26,404lb. Its maximum speed in level flight was Mach 0.98 at altitude. The F-102A Delta Dagger's span was 38ft 1.5in., length 68ft 4.5in., gross wing area 695sq ft, gross weight 28,150lb and maximum take-off weight 31,500lb. Its maximum speed was 825mph at 36,000ft, combat ceiling 51,800ft and service ceiling 53,400ft. The 'ultimate' F-106A Delta Dart had a span of 38ft 3.5in., a length of 70ft 9in., a gross wing area of 631.3sq ft and a gross weight of 33,370lb. The maximum speed of this interceptor was 1,525mph at 40,000ft and its service ceiling was around 57,000ft. Following on from the F-106, Convair proposed all manner of further developments and versions over several years, some having two engines and others fitted with new powerplants and canard foreplanes.

As previously noted in this volume, Fairey followed its Delta 2 with the Delta 3 long-range interceptor. The equivalent programme in the USA led to the North American F-108 Rapier, a very large aircraft that was abandoned before it flew. Convair did not submit an official proposal for the F-108 competition so, unlike Fairey, it never looked closely at a long-range interceptor follow-up.

The F-102A (known as the 'Deuce' in the frontline) first entered service with Air Defense Command in April 1956 as the first USAF delta-winged aircraft. In all 879 area-ruled F-102As were built, and there was also a TF-102A two-seat combat-proficiency trainer and tactical interceptor version. By pulling the original YF-102 design apart and re-engineering the airframe, Convair turned its Delta Dagger into an excellent combat aircraft. The F-106A, of which 277 were eventually manufactured, joined the USAF in 1959, and again a two-seat TF-106B trainer variant was also built. In the end the F-102 and F-106 proved to be very successful, long-serving aircraft, but the headaches suffered during their development had been tough going.

CHAPTER SIX

CONVAIR SEA DART

This final 'Convair' chapter looks at a unique project – a water-based fighter intended to operate at supersonic speeds. Several manufacturers worldwide have proposed such designs, but the Convair Sea Dart remains the only example to make it to flight-testing.

ADVANCED CONCEPT

By 1945, hydrodynamic research into flying boat hulls had indicated that lighter and aerodynamically clean shapes were now possible that would not suffer the severe stresses during alighting and take-off endured by conventional hulls. In addition, jet propulsion had brought the possibility of designing aircraft with a performance comparable to landplanes. In 1946, under a Bureau of Aeronautics (BuAer) contract, Convair began development of a high-speed fighter-type flying boat called the Skate. This featured a blended hull, a term indicating that the aircraft would ride so low in the water when at rest that its wings would assist in keeping it afloat.

Concurrently, NACA had taken a high-speed aircraft design and then attempted to incorporate acceptable hydrodynamic characteristics. This research included fitting simple ski-like surfaces called hydroskis to the underside of a model of the land-based Douglas D-558-2 Skyrocket research aircraft for water trials. Hydroskis operated as planing skis, and the resulting 1947 report indicated that they would be submerged when at rest or at very low speed, but would climb to the surface of the water for take-off. Indeed, they appeared to offer several advantages. The fuselage would not have to withstand the stresses of high-speed

The first Convair XF2Y-1 Sea Dart, BuNo 137634, pictured, it is thought, very early on in its career when the long nose probe was fitted. The seaplane fighter's original twin hydroski is well shown from this angle, as are the attachment struts. The forward pair were attached below the cockpit and the main pair level with the engine intakes. (Mark Aldrich Collection)

water operations, since at high speeds only the ski would be in contact with the water, and for flight the ski surface would retract into an aerodynamically clean fuselage. There was also a possibility that a ski could become a universal landing gear for use on water, snow, ice and sand – in fact on anything except a hard abrasive surface like a concrete runway.

In 1948 BuAer laid down a basic requirement for a seaplane fighter with a maximum speed of Mach 0.95 and capable of operating in five-foot high waves, Convair winning with a blended hull layout. However, by 1950, continued development saw the manufacturer produce a new design with twin hydroskis and a delta wing. This was designated Y2-2, and aerodynamically it was similar to the F-102 (in its original form) and had an estimated maximum speed of Mach 1.5 and a sea level rate of climb of 30,000ft per minute. Two examples were ordered in January 1951 as research aircraft powered by a pair of Westinghouse J46 engines, although two Westinghouse J34s would initially be used.

It was immediately apparent that this type of aircraft could provide air defence to a beachhead, thereby freeing an amphibious force from total dependence upon carrier aviation until landing fields were constructed. Other suggested uses included operations from an escort carrier (with a launch by catapult and then landing on the sea to taxi up a ramp back onto the ship) and the possibility of basing the aircraft aboard submarines (with take-offs and landings from the open sea). As a 'pantobased' machine, it could be treated in the same manner as a land-based fighter. It would be fully serviced on land and would simply taxi down the beach or ramp into the water for take-off. No clearing of the take-off path was necessary either, since floating obstructions would be deflected away by the high-planing pressure of the skis. F. Herbert Sharp was appointed project manager in February 1951 and Convair's aircraft was eventually named Sea Dart.

The basic design showed considerable promise and led, in August 1951, to the two Y2-2s being redesignated XF2Y-1s, indicating they were now fighter prototypes. In 1952–53 four YF2Y-1s, one static test article and 12 F2Y-1s, were ordered for evaluation. The four YF2Y-1s were classed as non-military so they could be built in the experimental shop to the same specification as the two XF2Y-1s. However, only one XF (BuNo 137634) and four YFs (BuNos 135762 through 135765) would be completed, and the third and fourth YF2Y-1s never received their engines and so never flew. The second XF2Y-1 received BuNo 137635 and the 12 F2Y-1s and static test article (itself originally a production airframe)

This extraordinary view shows how tightly the Sea Dart could be turned on relatively calm water. (Author's Collection)

BuNos 135766 to 135773
and 138530 to 138534.

The single-seat Sea
Dart's delta wing was swept
60 degrees at the leading edge,
it had a cropped delta fin,
and hydraulically operated
elevons and rudder on the
trailing edges. The wing
was continuous through the
fuselage to form a platform
on which to fix the engines
over the upper rear fuselage.
The hydroskis were aligned
to displace water outwards to
keep it away from the intakes,
and narrow anti-spray strakes

were also fitted on the sides of the forward fuselage. There was an
unusual V-shaped canopy with two flat glass panels, which proved
unsuitable from the points of view of visibility (insufficient light) and
from the need to eject in an emergency. Production airframes would
have received a different design.

The Sea Dart's body was built around a steel centreline keel and the
hull exhibited a fine aerodynamic form, with a 'V'-shaped underside.
The two hydroskis extended out on two oleo struts and retracted
after take-off to lie flush with the hull. The end fuselage formed a
streamlined section or ski that extended rearwards and underneath the
jet pipes. This would split symmetrically to provide braking both in the
water and during flight, and also differentially to operate as a rudder
when floating. When static in water, the Sea Dart sat with a two-degree
nose-up incidence to stop the wing leading edge from submerging. The
trailing edge then rested on the surface of the water, which enabled the
elevons to provide some lateral stability and a flat wake when moving.
On dry ground the nose-up angle was 17 degrees, and small wheels
were attached to the rear end of each ski and the ventral fin to enable
the Sea Dart to use engine thrust to taxi in and out of the water via a
ramp. There was also a towing dolly to help movement on land.

The production 'military' Sea Dart mock-up was reviewed in August
1952, and showed an armament of 44 2.75in. FFARs in packs of
22 tubes, one in each side of the forward fuselage. The tubes would
rotate outwards to fire hydraulically and then retract instantly once the
rockets had gone – an alternative armament was four 20mm cannon.
An APQ-50 electronic search radar and Aero 13E fire control system
were to be housed in the nose.

A rear view of BuNo 137634. The ski
wheels and the streamlined aft
fuselage section below and behind the
jet pipes can be clearly seen, the latter
serving as a split brake that could be
used both in the water and in the air.
Here, the nose probe has been
removed. (Mark Aldrich Collection)

SLOW START

Convair test pilot Sam Shannon began taxi trials in XF2Y-1 BuNo
137634 in San Diego Bay on 14 December 1952, the aircraft having
been completed early that month. On 14 January 1953 it left the water

and flew for about 1,000ft, but the official first flight did not take place until 9 April 1953 (with J34-WE-32 engines and no afterburner) due to difficulties with the hydroskis.

At speeds of 60mph and above, a phenomenon known as 'ski-pounding' had been encountered, the skis vibrating severely and threatening to damage the structure. This pounding came from the blunt or boat tail afterbody of the skis traversing wave patterns. The rougher the water, the worse it became. The combined vibration and pounding made conditions in the cockpit totally unacceptable when taking-off or landing, and pilots felt that the vibration would not be tolerated in a tactical aircraft.

Attempts to correct this condition included changing the ski shape and improving the shock absorbers between the aircraft and its skis. 'Ski-pounding' was never completely solved during the Sea Dart's career, but the problem was reduced somewhat by a redesign of the rear section of each hydroski.

For its initial water taxi tests, and possibly the first lift-offs, XF2Y-1 BuNo 137634 had a long nose boom fitted, which was later replaced by a short boom similar to what was installed in the YF2Y-1s. Testing of BuNo 137634 continued through the first half of 1954, most of the trials covering efforts to reduce the 'ski-pounding'. In due course, the J34s were replaced by more powerful afterburning XJ46-WE-2 units, for which there were also 'blow-in' doors aft of the intakes plus an extended rear fuselage to cover the engine to the end of the fin. In mid-1954 BuNo 137634 was grounded to have a single hydroski fitted.

Shannon was joined on the flying programme by Charles E. Richbourg, who, in early 1954, performed the maiden flight of BuNo 135762 – the first YF2Y-1 (it was originally to have been the second XF2Y-1). This machine was a little larger than BuNo 137634 and had J46-WE-2 engines to begin with. It also retained the twin-ski 'undercarriage' (the aircraft's skis were apparently shorter and broader than those fitted to the XF2Y-1), but lacked the additional wheels, which meant special beaching gear was required. This aircraft also featured longer chine strakes on its lower forward fuselage sides and, later, a small wing fence was added to each outboard upper wing surface

NEXT PAGES

THE SEA DART ON TAKE-OFF

This specially commissioned artwork from Adam Tooby shows the remarkable Convair XF2Y-1 Sea Dart prototype BuNo 137634 during one of its take-off runs for another test flight. The seaplane fighter was a rare breed in every respect. Very few proposals for such types have been made during the jet age, and just two have been flown in prototype form – the British Saunders-Roe SR.A/1, which made its maiden flight in 1947, and the Sea Dart. The bulky SR.A/1 was firmly subsonic, but Convair's design proved to be the only example of a water-based aircraft ever to exceed supersonic speed, which was achieved in a shallow dive on 3 August 1954. There were plans to build the Sea Dart in small production numbers, but in the end only five were built, four of which still survive today. In all, these machines completed 300 flights and test runs and made a very impressive sight, particularly during a take-off from the water with afterburners lit and spray everywhere. The Sea Dart was a truly remarkable machine, and it seems most unlikely that another seaplane fighter will ever be built.

(the only Sea Dart to have this feature).

BuNo 135762 was used to investigate the Sea Dart's high-speed performance and its aerodynamic stability and control characteristics. It also took part in open-sea trials, which were performed by both Richbourg and Shannon, the open-sea assessment taking place south of Point Loma, in San Diego. The trials involved considerable support, including the landing ship dock USS *Catamount* (LSD-17), a Douglas AD Skyraider chase aircraft, and a search and rescue helicopter. Richbourg performed all of BuNo 135762's flights through 1954, and on 3 August he made the Sea Dart the first (and only) water-based aircraft to exceed Mach 1 – a feat it achieved in a shallow dive at 34,000ft (the aircraft was incapable of level supersonic flight).

The XF2Y-1 takes off from San Diego Bay, the US Navy's most active Pacific coast port. Consequently, Sea Dart pilots had to take extra care looking out for other traffic both on the water and in the air. (Mark Nankivil Collection)

Tragically, on 4 November 1954, Richbourg died when BuNo 135762 disintegrated in mid-air at low level during a press demonstration of the US Navy's Mobile Base Concept in San Diego. Whilst flying at around 575mph, the aircraft inadvertently entered a pilot-induced divergent longitudinal pitch oscillation and broke up. The oscillation, which exceeded the aircraft's structural limit, was caused by a combination of high speed at low level – the Sea Dart's early hydraulic flight control system had not matured sufficiently to handle the high dynamic pressures encountered at such speeds at low level. This loss had nothing to do with any design flaws in the aircraft, or because the Sea Dart was a seaplane. Nevertheless, all flying was immediately suspended, and the type would never again reach such speeds in flight.

The second YF2Y-1, BuNo 135763 and the last Sea Dart to fly, made its maiden flight on 4 March 1955. It was the same as BuNo 135762 except for the configuration of the twin-ski afterbody, which was tapered and re-introduced wheels. Pilot for the aircraft's initial taxi and take-off tests was Billy Jack 'BJ' Long, who had joined the test team in December 1954 having previously flown in chase aircraft. Long subsequently became the most experienced Sea Dart pilot, and this aircraft would evaluate the changes made to the twin-ski format and perform further open-sea operations.

The trials showed that the modified twin-ski arrangement was still unsatisfactory, with the 'ski-pounding' vibration and wave action in the open sea still too much for both aircrew and airframe. It was hoped the discomfort might be reduced when four 1,000lb thrust rocket-assisted take-off bottles were installed beneath BuNo 135763's wings, the extra power reducing the take-off run. Twin-ski testing, and BuNo 135763's brief flying career, came to an end on 28 April 1955.

The first YF2Y-1, BuNo 135762, takes off from San Diego Bay. Judging by the volume of spray created in the seaplane fighter's wake, this must have been spectacular to watch. The engines were fed air via D-shaped intakes. (Mark Nankivil Collection)

This view looking down on BuNo 135762 shows how the wing trailing edges were slightly cropped near the tip. The yellow stripes on the fin, rudder, wings and around the air intakes were applied to assist in the interpretation of photographs of the aircraft's attitude taken during take-offs and landings. The rest of the airframe was painted blue. (Terry Panopalis Collection)

IN CONTROL

Long has described in print what the Sea Dart was like to handle in the air and on water. On take-off and landing the sequences were pretty well the same for both twin and single-ski arrangements. When taxiing on idle power, its speed over water was 2.3 to 3.5mph, but opening the lower fuselage speed brakes and extending the skis would reduce this to just 1.15 to 2.3mph. Take-off initially required the skis to be fully extended and with just military (dry) power from the engines. The two skis and the tail 'ski' would form a stable tripod, and the speed at which the Sea Dart would begin to plane was 9.2 to 11.5mph. At this point the skis were moved to the intermediate position and reheat was introduced to begin the acceleration.

The aircraft would rise onto the 'hump' (the point of maximum water resistance) at 40 to 46mph and, since the centre of gravity lay behind the skis, the Sea Dart would assume its natural attitude during the take-off run. The skis would be returned to their fully extended position for the lift-off, and on reaching about 145mph the nose would be rotated sharply to allow the aircraft to leave the water. The skis would then be retracted into the hull. After being refitted with a single ski, the XF2Y-1 was only flown at low speeds, with the ski remaining slightly extended. It was, nevertheless, aerodynamically clean.

Once airborne, the Sea Dart was considered pleasant to fly, and in general pilots seemed to enjoy flying it. In fact, those members of the evaluation team who were seaplane pilots liked the delta wing because they did not have to worry about wingtip floats digging in and causing water-loops – a problem experienced by all seaplanes then in service. However, the aircraft was underpowered, and its rate of climb and acceleration proved unsatisfactory. Landings were made at a speed of 138mph and with the hydroskis fully extended throughout. After touching down on the surface of the water, the machine would decelerate rapidly and, when the speed fell to about 6mph, the skis could be retracted to their beaching position in readiness for the Sea Dart to taxi back to its base.

Standard procedure for take-off and landing was to adopt a heading parallel to any major wave or swell condition, whilst also heading into wind as much as possible. It was rare for an engine to flame-out from ingesting water, but if this did happen it became impossible to taxi in a straight line because of the asymmetric thrust from the remaining engine. As previously noted, the refined twin-skis reduced the 'pounding' problem, but never eliminated it. Nevertheless, their hydrodynamic stability and control were described as 'excellent'.

During the flying programme the power output of the Westinghouse J46-WE-2 engine fell well short of expectations, with the aircraft's estimated maximum speed now Mach 0.99 rather than the hoped for Mach 1.5. This loss was also attributed to aerodynamic deficiencies in the airframe, not dissimilar in fact to the F-102 in the previous chapter (the Sea Dart was not subject to 'area ruling'). These development problems, coupled with a funding shortage, brought about the cancellation of the F2Y-1 order. The money thus recovered was used instead to build carrier-based Vought F8U-1 Crusader fighters.

The first XF2Y-1 flies over San Diego during a test flight. Both this aircraft and the first YF2Y-1 did not wear national insignia. Note the yellow applied to the underside of the wings. (Terry Panopalis Collection)

Another factor that held back the Sea Dart's flight development was corrosion. The availability of the aircraft in general due to maintenance problems was described as 'very poor' and the biggest factor here was salt water corrosion. In fact, Convair had waterproofed the fuselage to only a few inches above the static waterline, which allowed spray to seep in onto equipment. There was no corrosion protection for the fuel metering, fire warning system or afterburner controls, and magnesium had been used

The second XF2Y-1, BuNo 135762, taxies away from the Convair seaplane ramp across a smooth San Diego Bay prior to taking off on another test flight. Painted dark blue overall, this Sea Dart did carry national insignia. The waterline is level with the wing trailing edge and the elevons. After entering the water, the ski wheels would be rotated through 90 degrees to enable the ski's tapered afterbody to be in the correct hydrodynamic position. (Mark Nankivil Collection)

for some structural parts. This, coupled with the fact that water had ingested through the jet tailpipe, and the use of magnesium castings in the engine, was seen as a 'built-in maintenance problem'.

The J46 engines also suffered from the effects of salt water in a different way. Salt particles from the atmosphere would collect and become baked onto the engine compressor and stator blades, in the process reducing thrust and even causing compressor stall on selection of high power and afterburning. The solution was to fit a 20-gallon fresh water tank in both surviving airframes to enable small quantities of water to be injected into the engine air intake area just before take-off or when the engines were running at idle. This proved very successful in washing the salt contamination away and restoring full power.

SINGLE HYDROSKI

During the second half of 1954 XF2Y-1 BuNo 137634 had its original hydroskis replaced by a large single centrally-mounted ski which, though not fully retractable, could be raised and lowered to a degree. In section, it took the form of a shallow 'V', and was attached by four struts. Twin wheels were fitted at its rear end. The ski was very rigid, it had a ten-degree deadrise (the angle measurement between the boat bottom and a horizontal plane on either side of the centre keel), and the afterbody was tapered to assist with water penetration – landings were made with the ski fully extended. This fitting was for hydroski research only, and would not involve any high-speed flight or aerodynamic testing.

The initial trials began in late autumn 1954, and were conducted by both Shannon and Richbourg, who immediately experienced unacceptable hydrodynamic stability and control. The 'ski-pounding' was much reduced, but there were new problems with 'porpoising' (divergent pitch oscillation) that saw take-off runs sometimes having to be aborted at speeds ranging between 46 to 57mph. However, corrective actions, including a variable damping system, proved promising enough for the US Navy to schedule its preliminary Sea Dart evaluation for November 1954. The loss of Richbourg and the first YF2Y-1 then saw the evaluation postponed until May 1955. When conducted, it confirmed that the single hydroski was much better hydrodynamically than the twin format, but

XF2Y-1 BuNo 137634 was grounded in mid-1954 to have the single hydroski fitted, which is seen here in the extended position. In the wake of this modification the XF2Y-1 was only flown at low speeds, with the ski remaining slightly extended. (Terry Panopalis Collection)

at this stage its take-off stability was poor and it still had a tendency to porpoise. It was this evaluation that made the Chief of Naval Operations, in January 1956, finally recommend against further procurement of the Sea Dart, and to cancel the Operational Requirement. The Sea Dart was now just a hydrodynamic research vehicle.

Gradually, however, the single-ski's performance was improved. Once the lateral control deflection of the elevons had been doubled, the directional stability and control were described as excellent. Good hydrodynamic stability and control characteristics had at last been established, vibration was not present with the final single-ski configuration, and the 'pounding' loads were now acceptable and simply proportional to how rough the water was. The spray characteristics were still poor but the single hydroski was, without question, the superior of the two types.

Long conducted the XF2Y-1's last open-sea test on 16 January 1956 in an attempt to establish the single-ski's upper limits for operating in rough seas. With waves between six and ten feet high, plus a 23mph wind, the aircraft took a battering on both take-off and landing – the former including vicious porpoising and 8.5g wave impacts before the pilot was able to clear the water safely. This proved to be the last flight made by a Sea Dart, the single-ski programme having been completed. The two aircraft duly went into storage.

However, in late 1956, BuAer opened a new trials programme for a much smaller, fixed, hydroski on the XF2Y-1 which, besides having planing ski capabilities, had a hydrofoil shape. Although it generated hydrodynamic lift, the new ski's shape and its short struts made take-offs impossible. Long conducted three tests with this arrangement in April 1957, the last on the 8th, and found that severe pounding and discomfort in the cockpit prevented him from travelling over the water at more than 57–69 knots.

Although this design was abandoned, BuAer came back with another rigid ski layout in the autumn of 1957. The new form was similar to the earlier rigid hydrofoil-shaped ski but about half the size (about 20 per cent of Convair's original single ski). It was tested on BuNo 137634 by Convair test pilot Donald P. Germeraad, but again gave an unacceptable performance.

During their careers, the three Sea Darts accumulated 300 flights and test runs, 250 of which were conducted by the XF2Y-1. From mid-1952 Convair worked on a single-engined development called the F2Y-2. Powered by a Wright J67, this was expected to be supersonic at sea level and to exceed Mach 2 at height, but it was not built. In 1962, America's military aircraft designations were rearranged into one system and, despite not having operated since 1957, the Sea Dart was redesignated F-7. The YF2Y-1 was changed to YF-7A and the F2Y-1 to F-7A.

The large single hydroski fitted to the Sea Dart eventually worked well, and the programme overall proved the feasibility of a supersonic water-based fighter for naval operations. But the various development problems, a lack of available funds after the end of the Korean War, and the US Navy's desire to build large carriers helped kill the project. The four surviving Sea Darts all still exist. XF2Y-1 BuNo 137634 is at the Smithsonian Institution in Washington, D.C., and YF2Y-1 BuNo 135763 is on display at the entrance to the San Diego Air & Space Museum. The second YF2Y-1, BuNo 135764, resides at the Wings of Freedom Museum at Willow Grove, Pennsylvania, and BuNo 135765 is on show at the Florida Air Museum at Lakeland Linder Airport.

CONVAIR X/YF2Y-1 SEA DART	
Wing span	XF2Y-1 30ft 6in., YF2Y-1 33ft 8in.
Length	YF2Y-1 51ft 1.5in.
Wing Area	XF2Y-1 539sq ft, YF2Y-1 568sq ft
Loaded Weight	XF2Y-1 15,000lb, YF2Y-1 16,527lb
Maximum Take-off Weight	YF2Y-1 21,500lb
Internal Fuel Capacity	6,542lb
Estimated Performance (YF2Y-1)	
Maximum Speed	695mph at 8,000ft and 825mph at 35,000ft
Initial Rate of Climb	17,100ft per minute
Service ceiling	54,800ft
Range	513 miles
Airframe Limits (YF2Y-1)	
Vne (never-exceed speed)	402mph IAS below 20,000ft, Mach 1.05 above 20,000ft
Ski Retraction/Extension Limits	in flight 207mph IAS, on water 6mph
Powerplant	
XF2Y-1 (initial)	two Westinghouse J34-WE-32 turbojets, each rated at 3,250lb thrust dry and 4,200lb thrust with afterburning
XF2Y-1 (final) and YF2Y-1	two Westinghouse XJ46-WE-2 turbojets, each rated at 4,080lb thrust dry and 6,100lb thrust with afterburning

CHAPTER SEVEN

AVRO 707 SERIES

Two of the aircraft that formed the British V-bomber force during the 1950s, the Avro Vulcan and Handley Page Victor, introduced very advanced wing shapes – the delta wing and crescent wing, respectively. In fact, these wing forms were so advanced for the late 1940s that, when prototypes of both bombers were first planned, it was considered prudent to build scale-model aeroplanes to assess their flying characteristics. The Victor was preceded by the short-lived HP.88 research aircraft and the Vulcan by the first Avro 707. The latter series was subsequently expanded and eventually reached a total of five airframes. Since these aircraft were designed and built for bomber 'applications', they make an interesting comparison to the other types described in this book.

An excellent side view of the first, and short-lived, Avro 707 prototype VX784 in September 1949. The aircraft was fitted with a Gloster Meteor F3 cockpit and nose wheel, and, overall, presented a short and stocky appearance. The pilot, however, had a superb view out. (Author's Collection)

AVRO 707 AND 710

After a design competition held against Specification B.35/46, two Avro 698 bomber prototypes were ordered in June 1948 (the type was christened Vulcan in October 1952). Avro also proposed to build some scale-model aircraft to assess the delta wing, and these were ordered at the same time. Two Avro 707 one-third-scale aircraft (serials VX784 and VX790) would conduct research into the delta's flight characteristics at low speeds and heights, and two half-scale Type 710s would undertake equivalent assessments at high Mach numbers and altitudes. The two 710s were cancelled in February 1949 because they would absorb too much of Avro's available design capacity. The 707s were far more important anyway because if any low-speed/low-altitude control and stability problems were not solved then the bomber's high-speed qualities would become insignificant.

Although the 707s were initially to be built mostly in wood and use a lot of existing equipment, their structure was soon changed to all-metal. A welded steel tube assembly was covered by unstressed aluminium alloy sheet panels, while the wings had a two-spar structure and were fitted with four control surfaces on the trailing edge, two inboard elevators and two outboard ailerons. The fin also employed a two-spar structure, and in front of it there was a bifurcated (i.e. divided on the centreline) air intake positioned saddle-fashion in the uppersurface of the fuselage that fed a Rolls-Royce Derwent jet engine. A Gloster Meteor F3 fighter cockpit and nose wheel and the undercarriage from the limited-run Avro Athena advanced trainer were all fitted to save time and money. None of the five 707s would have a pressurised cockpit, and VX784 (and VX790, which followed) had a single fuel tank in the rear fuselage. The first 707 was designed and built in only 14 months. Critically, however, it had no ejection seat.

The two 707s were covered by Specification E.15/48 of October 1948, and were intended to explore the flight envelope up to a speed of around 500mph. A key secondary role would be the investigation of flight at the high angles of incidence necessary for a delta-winged aircraft to take off and land. Having completed taxi trials at its birthplace, Woodford, Greater Manchester, VX784 was taken to Boscombe Down. On 3 September 1949 it made a short hop, and the following day the 707 was taken aloft (in the process becoming only the second jet-powered delta-wing aircraft in the world to fly after the XF-92A) for the first time by Avro test pilot Flt Lt Eric 'Red' Esler.

Over the next week VX784 accumulated around three hours of flight time, during which the handling characteristics proved to be quite satisfactory. This also qualified the aircraft for static display at that month's SBAC Farnborough Airshow. The 707's arrival there, very much as a 'dark horse', caused something of a sensation since it presented (in *Flight* magazine's words) 'a things-to-come appearance the like of which has never before been seen in this country'. On his arrival, Esler made two circuits of wide radius and then flew along the

VX784 on short-finals, either at Boscombe Down or Farnborough, in September 1949. Note the underwing flaps deployed for landing. (Avro Heritage)

runway at 300–350mph at an altitude of around 600ft, before entering the landing circuit. He then made a long, straight, low approach, before touching down at what seemed to be something over 115mph.

However, the 707 would have little opportunity to explore its flight envelope. On 30 September 1949 VX784 was destroyed when it flew into the ground near Blackbushe Aerodrome seven minutes after taking off from RAE Farnborough for a handling check flight (some adjustments had just been made to the ailerons). Tragically, Esler was killed. At the end of its descent the aircraft had crashed in a very slight tail-down attitude, and both the centre fuselage and nose were burnt out. The cause of the accident is still not entirely clear today, but prior to the crash VX784 had been flying at a low speed and altitude, and its fuselage-mounted braking flaps (airbrakes) were about one-third open at the time. It is possible that the high level of additional drag these created may have produced a very high rate of descent, with insufficient time for the pilot to recover. Poor weather conditions may have also been a factor in the accident. No structural or engine failure had occurred, so it seemed most probable that the wing brakes had contributed to the tragedy.

The cause of the accident was in no way traceable to the delta configuration, but after the accident enquiry, the 707 airframes that followed were fitted with a set of retractable and mechanically interconnected airbrakes attached to both the top and bottom wing surfaces. Had Esler been given an ejection seat, he might have survived. Having joined Avro in June 1948, he had been made responsible for all flying of the 707.

AVRO 707B

Following the accident, a decision was taken to build two more 707s, the second machine, VX790, and now a third, WD280 – the latter

The Avro 707B VX790, with its 'P' prototype marking and Hawker Siddeley Group insignia on the nose, photographed almost certainly at Boscombe Down. (Avro Heritage)

VX790 presents underside detail during a flypast at the SBAC Farnborough Airshow of 1951. This aircraft was used to investigate the low-speed stability of delta wings. Note the length and complexity of the nose probe. (Author's Collection)

This air-to-air photograph of VX790 clearly shows the aircraft's ventral air intake positioned, somewhat unusually, over the rear fuselage. This is the larger, raised, air intake form that was fitted later in the aircraft's career. (Avro Heritage)

aircraft is described later in this chapter. Both airframes were quite different to their predecessor. VX790 retained the original wing design and structure, and the same main undercarriage, but now introduced balanced elevators, modified airbrakes and a redesigned cockpit, complete with a Martin-Baker ejection seat. It also had an all-monocoque nose structure that was 2ft 6in. longer in order to improve the aerodynamics and centre of gravity, plus a 12in. extension to the top of the fin. Finally, a modified nose leg oleo from a Hawker Sea Hawk fighter was fitted and extended by nine inches to provide a better angle-of-incidence during take-offs.

An important factor revealed by the 707 that would apply to the Vulcan as well, and which might otherwise have remained undetected for some time, was the precise relationship between the angle of wing incidence and the speed at which the nose wheel could be lifted off the runway during the take-off run. VX784 had had to reach almost unstick speed before its nose wheel could be raised clear of the ground, causing the aeroplane to 'jump' off the ground abruptly. The take-off run was also quite long. This shortcoming was dealt with on VX790 by the extended nose gear leg and wing incidence, whereupon it became possible to lift the nose at less than 80 per cent of the unstick speed. The nose leg extension also appeared on the Vulcan.

In its new form, the aircraft was redesignated Avro 707B, and VX790 made its maiden flight from Boscombe Down, flown by Avro's new superintendent of flying, Wg Cdr R. J. 'Roly' Falk, on 6 September 1950. Like VX784 the previous year, the 707B almost immediately went to the SBAC Farnborough Airshow, before starting a prolonged spell of research flying from Dunsfold, in Surrey.

One factor shown up during this programme was that disturbed airflow produced at higher speeds by the cockpit canopy would affect the air entering the intake, causing partial engine starvation. This was countered by a structural modification that saw the introduction of a substantial 'hump' to the aircraft's back and the addition of a NACA divergent ramp to provide better pressure recovery. This work took place during February 1951, and the

AVRO 707B

Avro 707B VX790 was flown in this overall gloss blue scheme, complete
with Hawker Siddeley Group insignia beneath the cockpit, from 1951.

new arrangement improved the airflow to the engine in all regimes,
and especially so at high AoA. However, this modification was not
relevant to the Vulcan, and delayed the latter's development.

In due course, Avro established a self-contained team at Boscombe
Down to handle its delta research flying, and VX790 was able to show
that, when airborne, a tailless aeroplane could have entirely satisfactory
qualities at all speeds between the stall at 94mph up to a maximum
speed of 438mph. However, an undamped pitching oscillation
appeared that was traced to an out-of-phase elevator motion, and this
was just enough to produce a destabilising pitching moment. This
quite undesirable feature was almost eliminated by fitting spring tab
controls on the 707A (the bomber prototype had irreversible controls,
which obviated its presence on the Vulcan).

On 21 September 1951 VX790 experienced a landing accident at
Boscombe Down in which its pilot, Wg Cdr Thomas Balmforth, was
injured. After having touched down, the aircraft left the ground in a
very high nose-up attitude, a wing then dropped and hit the ground
and this slewed the airframe around and damaged its nose. After repair
at Woodford, VX790 returned to flight in mid-1952 and attended the
September SBAC Farnborough Airshow, before being transferred to
RAE Farnborough immediately afterwards.

Another discovery made with VX790 that subsequently benefited
the Vulcan was that by adjusting the line of action of the propelling
nozzle (i.e. tilting the jet exhaust both outwards and downwards),
variations of longitudinal stability and trim with changes in engine
thrust were virtually eliminated both with the 707 and the bomber.
On the Vulcan (which had a pair of Bristol Olympus engines in each
wing root), the inboard jet nozzles were angled downwards through
four to five degrees until any change in thrust had almost no effect on
trim. At the same time, the outboard nozzles were turned through the
same angle and rotated.

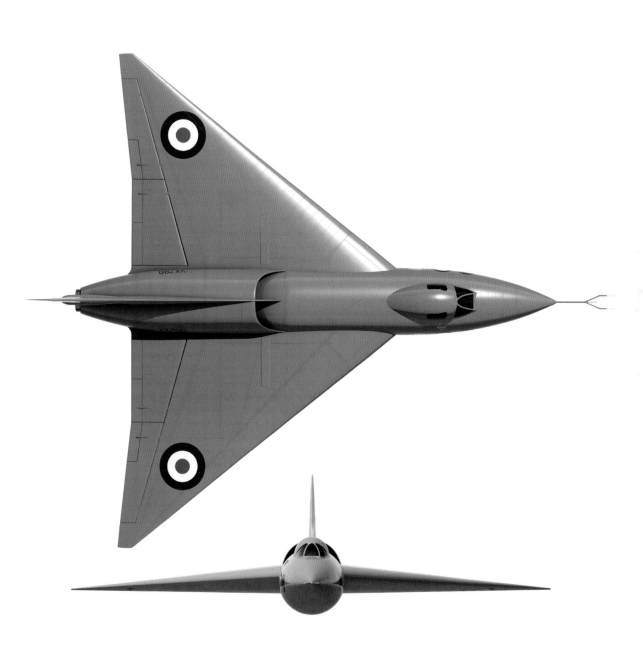

X PLANES
AVRO 707B

This change produced a worthwhile reduction in engine-out speed, while the yawing moment created by an outer engine became the same as that produced by its neighbouring inner unit. As a result, the size of the bomber's vertical tail could be reduced. These changes were all made possible using 707 flight data.

In January 1956 VX790 joined the Empire Test Pilots' School at Farnborough, although its flying career came to an end on 25 September that same year following a second landing accident. It was Struck Off Charge for use as a source of spare parts in November 1957 and scrapped in 1960.

The gap left by the cancellation of the 'high-speed' 710 was filled by a 'high-speed' 707 and new Specification E.10/49 of July 1949, which requested a maximum speed of not less than 575mph at 36,000ft and a dive speed limit of Mach 0.95. The new version was designated 707A, and two examples were ordered with serials WD280 and WZ736.

The 707A was far more representative of the full-scale bomber because, although the forward fuselage ahead of the main spar attachment frame and both the fin and rudder were identical to VX790, there was a new wing with the engine now fed through wing root air intakes. In addition, bar a small portion inboard that featured a new and separate dive recovery flap, all of the wing trailing edge had a modest amount of sweepback. The 707B's shrouded control surfaces, with geared tabs, had also given way to internal sealed balances with spring tab controls, the aileron area was reduced, with the latter now also carried through to the squared-off wingtips, and inboard of the ailerons were flaps for trim and dive-recovery. Finally, the point of maximum thickness in the wing profile had been swept forward at the roots, and a Derwent 8 engine of slightly increased thrust was installed.

To begin with, WD280 had manual controls, but after stability problems had been experienced the aircraft was retro-fitted with fully powered irreversible controls on both elevators and ailerons.

WD280 was constructed at Woodford and Roly Falk took the aircraft on its maiden flight, from Boscombe Down, on 14 June 1951. Between 30 June and 4 July 1952 the first 707A took part in the CFE's Annual Convention at West Raynham, and then in September it appeared at the SBAC Farnborough Airshow. Another public display followed at the Paris Air Show of July 1953. After this, WD280 was used by RAE Farnborough, and then from October 1953 for delta wing experiments by Avro itself at Woodford.

This particular member of the 707 family influenced the Vulcan bomber programme in one very important area. Test flying with both WD280 and the bomber prototypes revealed that applying g at high altitudes and high speed could generate minor buffeting and a pronounced wing 'buzz' (a high-frequency vibration). Although this was not a serious problem, it could affect the fatigue life of the outer wings. In addition, further in-flight investigations indicated that this buffet regime came uncomfortably close to the performance boundary expected with later developments of the Vulcan (which would have more powerful engines installed).

The first 707A, WD280 was fitted with extensions to the wing leading edges – an alteration that would also find its way to the Vulcan. (Author's Collection)

The second 707A was WZ736. Comparison with the side view of the original 707, VX784, shows the considerable degree of development and change made on these later machines. There were three control surfaces along each wing trailing edge – from inboard to outboard, dive recovery flaps, elevators and ailerons. (Avro Heritage)

Adding wing fences did not solve the problem, but a kink introduced on the outer portion of the wing leading edge eliminated it completely. The inner part of the outer wing had its sweep angle reduced, while the outermost portion was swept rather more. In fact, a 20 per cent chord extension was added over the outer wing leading edge, and this extension was then reduced to zero at about 50 per cent semi-span. Flight trials of this modified wing were conducted with WD280 after it had been refitted at Bracebridge Heath – the home of Avro's repair and overhaul facility in Lincolnshire. The modification was transferred to the Vulcan itself in early 1955.

In 1956 WD280 was shipped to Australia on board the aircraft carrier HMAS *Melbourne* to begin a new role operating with the Commonwealth Aeronautical Advisory Research Council. The aircraft was based at RAAF Laverton, in Victoria, and this work lasted until 1961. The main project was an examination of the airflow over a delta wing at low speeds, which, at one stage, involved applying grit of varying coarseness to the underside of the wing (this improved both elevator and aileron effectiveness and produced better control). WD280 was finally Struck Off Charge in February 1967.

The second 707A, WZ736, was ordered specifically at the request of the RAE for general research work. Built at Bracebridge Heath, it was taken by road to RAF Waddington, in Lincolnshire, for its maiden flight, which took place on 20 February 1953. The aircraft joined RAE Farnborough in June 1953 and was used initially in the development of an automatic throttle system.

In September 1955 WZ736 was moved to the National Aeronautical Establishment at Bedford to take part in trials with an 'automatic approach' system, a role which also saw the aircraft perform automatic landing trials with the Armament and Instrument Experimental

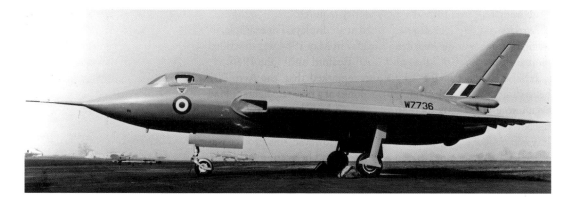

Establishment at Martlesham Heath, in Suffolk, both in November of that year and again in 1956. July 1957 brought further trials at Bedford. Finally, in May 1962, WZ736 was returned to Farnborough, where the aircraft was eventually Struck Off Charge so that it could provide spares to keep WZ744 flying.

TWO-SEATER 707C

The final 707 variant introduced twin side-by-side seating. Although not strictly a trainer, this dual-control aircraft would prove invaluable in providing pilots with experience in handling delta-winged aeroplanes. Known as the 707C, plans were originally drawn up to build four such airframes – Specification E.10/49 Issue 2 was duly written around the type in November 1951, but only one was built, WZ744. The solitary change from the second 707A airframe was the new broader cockpit enclosure, which was so cramped that there was no space for ejection seats. It also had circular side windows that offered a relatively poor sideways view.

WZ744 was assembled at Bracebridge Heath and Sqn Ldr T. B. Wales took the aircraft on its maiden flight, from Waddington, on 1 July 1953. It then went to A&AEE Boscombe Down to provide aircrew with general appreciation flying and pilot familiarisation on delta-winged aeroplanes. It was also used for comparative gun-aiming trials before, in September 1956, being returned to Avro's Woodford factory to be fitted out with instrumentation for electrically controlled signalling. On joining RAE Bedford, WZ744 conducted some of the earliest work undertaken using fly-by-wire electric servo control systems, this new installation having duplicated the normal control circuits.

In its 22 March 1962 issue, *Flight* magazine described WZ744's involvement with electrically signalled flight controls, which had been developed by RAE Farnborough:

'Such a system can overcome the disadvantages of mechanically-signalled controls in very large aircraft, and also allows the application of a manoeuvre demand system to provide aircraft responses largely independent of flight conditions. Boulton Paul applied electrical signalling to the Tay-Viscount some years ago. The 707C is being used to investigate the characteristics to be preferred in a manoeuvre demand system, and to prove the integrity required.'

On occasion, WZ744 also performed at air displays. For example, its roll performance at the Yeovilton Air Day in May 1954 was described as 'beautiful'. The 707C flew with RAE Bedford until June 1966.

Press statements in the 1950s also remarked that 'the Avro 707 research aircraft appears to have the makings of a first-rate fighter'. Had events gone differently there would indeed have been an Avro delta fighter. In fact, the Avro 720 delta-winged, rocket-powered, fighter/interceptor was developed from the 707. However, this project was cancelled in 1955 before the first prototype had been completed.

Although VX784 remained unpainted during its brief existence, the remaining four 707s were adorned with very bright colour schemes.

The solitary 707C, WZ744, featured a wider two-seat, side-by-side, cockpit. Here, its airbrakes are fully deployed to allow the aircraft to remain in formation with the slower photo-aircraft. Note the matt black anti-glare panel in front of the canopy. This photograph would have been taken for recognition purposes while the 707C was flying from Boscombe Down. (Author's Collection)

VX790 appeared in a gloss blue livery, WD280 started its career in salmon pink but subsequently switched to a bright red scheme, WZ736 was at first a glossy orange but later received a yellow scheme with a black trim, and WZ744 was painted silver, with a matt black anti-glare panel ahead of the cockpit. The SBAC Farnborough Airshow of September 1953 saw all four 707s perform a wonderful combined flypast with the two all-white Vulcan prototypes – event commentator Maj Oliver Stewart was heard to say 'which Vulcan uses Persil?!'

Three examples still survive today – fittingly, WD280 is preserved in Australia at the RAAF Museum at Point Cook, Victoria, WZ736 is displayed at the Museum of Science and Industry in Manchester and WZ744 is part of the RAF Museum collection at Cosford.

One flaw of the early 707s was that they were not direct replicas of the bomber for which they were designed to provide data. For example, the manual controls were a problem and consumed valuable development time when the bomber used powered controls (the final three 707s received powered controls retrospectively). In addition, the dorsal intake had no relevance to the Vulcan, and yet needed modifications of its own to make it function better. But these criticisms were more than balanced by the subsequent work performed by this series of aeroplanes.

The main benefits derived by the Vulcan (which first flew on 30 August 1952) from the 707s were the extended nose leg, compound-sweep wing and the tilting of the jet exhaust. In summary, these small research aircraft did not provide as much support to the Vulcan programme as Avro had hoped they would, but because they were found to be capable of collecting data quite rapidly, the 707s proved ideal for aeronautical research in general.

In a late January 1958 issue, *Flight* summarised one point that showed how successful the delta had been for this family of aeroplanes:

'One of the most remarkable characteristics of the subsonic delta wing developed for the 698 [Vulcan] was found to be that, when its angle-of-attack was progressively increased, no sudden loss of lift occurred, as is suffered at the stalling point of a conventional wing. Tunnel testing with the 707 was conducted at angles of attack up to 60 degrees, and even at this fantastic inclination the lift was still approximately 90 per cent of the maximum value.'

The Fairey Delta 1 and Convair XF-92A were essentially trailblazers for the delta wing in their respective countries, and both were followed by supersonic developments where speed and climb performance were what mattered most. Indeed, both the Delta 2 and F-102 could only fulfil their function if they could achieve well in excess of Mach 1. In comparison, the objective of the series of Avro 707s was to confirm and 'mature' the delta's flight characteristics to provide an excellent performance over the speed range from take-off and landing up to high subsonic speeds. Sadly, there was no production fighter from Fairey, but the Delta Dagger, Delta Dart and the Vulcan served their countries well, and the knowledge gained from these programmes found its way into later products, not least the Concorde supersonic airliner and Convair's B-58 Hustler bomber.

AVRO 707			
Powerplant			
707 and 707B		One 3,500lb thrust Rolls-Royce Derwent 5	
707A and 707C		One 3,600lb thrust Rolls-Royce Derwent 8	
Dimensions			
	Span	**Length**	**Gross Wing Area**
707	33ft 0in.	40ft 2.25in.	366.5sq ft
707B	33ft 0in.	41ft 3.5in.	366.5sq ft
707A and 707C	34ft 2in.	42ft 4in.	408sq ft
Wing thickness/chord ratio (VX784 and VX790)		10 per cent constant	
Gross Weight			
707	8,600lb		
707B	9,500lb		
707A	9,800lb		
707C	10,000lb		
Maximum Level Speed			
707B	438mph		
707A and 707C	403mph		

FURTHER READING

Allen, Francis, *Sea-Skimming Predator – Convair's Fabulous Sea Dart*, Air Enthusiast Issue 102 (November/December 2002)

Alling, Frederick, *The F-102 Airplane, 1950–1956*, Air Material Command Historical Study 310 (1957)

Bradley, Robert E., *The Birth of the Delta Wing*, Journal of the American Aviation Historical Society (Winter 2003)

Bradley, Robert E., *Convair Advanced Designs II – Secret Fighters, Attack Aircraft and Concepts 1929–1973*, Crécy Publishing (2013)

Buttler, Tony, *Early US Jet Fighters – Proposals, Projects and Prototypes*, Hikoki Publications (2013)

Buttler, Tony, *British Secret Projects – Jet Fighters since 1950*, Crécy Publishing (2017)

Buttler, Tony and Delezenne, Jean-Louis, *X-Planes of Europe – Secret Research Aircraft from the Golden Age 1946–1974*, Hikoki Publications (2010)

Desoutter, D. M., *Aircraft and Missiles*, Faber and Faber (1959)

Donald, David, *Convair F2Y Sea Dart Supersonic Seaplane*, International Air Power Review Volume 12 (2004)

Dorr, Robert F., *Convair F-102 Delta Dagger*, Wings of Fame Volume 17 (1999)

Jenkins, Dennis R. and Landis, Tony R., *Experimental & Prototype US Air Force Jet Fighters*, Specialty Press (2008)

Knaack, Marcelle Size, *Post-World War II Fighters 1945–1973*, Office of Air Force History (1986)

Long, B. J., *Sea Dart – USN XF2Y-1 and YF2Y-1*, Society of Experimental Test Pilots Report (1979)

Long, B. J., *Sea Dart – US Navy XF2Y-1 and YF2Y-1 Experimental Supersonic Seaplanes*, Journal of the American Aviation Historical Society (Spring 1979)

Matthews, Henry, *Convair XF-92A Dart Delta Wing Research Aircraft*, World X-Planes Past, Present and Future, Issue 1 (2005)

Matthews, Henry and Davison, Peter, *The Speed Saga: FD-2 and BAC.221 – The Complete History*, HPM Publications (2006)

Morrow, Ardath M., *Case History of the XF-92*, Air Material Command Historical Office (June 1949)

Other sources consulted included the *Flightglobal Archive* website (*Flight* magazine archive), original Fairey and Air Ministry documents in the British National Archives at Kew, original NACA reports from the USA, and reports from the US National Archives at College Park, Maryland.

INDEX

Page numbers in **bold** refer to illustrations and their caption.